GISLEBERTVS · HOC FECIT

SCULPTOR OF AUTUN

DENIS GRIVOT AND GEORGE ZARNECKI

introduction by T. S. R. BOASE, **President of Magdalen College, Oxford**

HACKER ART BOOKS  NEW YORK 1985

Christ in majesty (detail of tympanum)

Omnia dispono solus meritos corono
quos scelus exercet me judice poena coercet
*I alone dispose of all things and crown the just,
Those who follow crime I judge and punish.*

In Memoriam
Peter Kendal Bushe (1929-1960)
friend and colleague, without whom
this book would not have been published
A.F.

First published 1961, New York

Reissued 1985 by Hacker Art Books, New York

Library of Congress Catalogue Card Number 84-80599
International Standard Book Number 0-87817-296-3

Printed in the United States of America

1

2

Contents

The illustrations have for the most part been grouped with the chapters describing them, and are indicated in italics above. Detailed lists of the *tympanum*, the *capitals* and the *north doorway*, together with the relevant plans, have been printed immediately before or after the plates themselves for ease of reference. The list of *capitals* has been printed on a fold-out page (p. 144) so that it can be consulted at the same time as the plates.

A detailed list of the *documentary and comparative plates (a-m, Ⓐ-Ⓓ)* is given on the following page.

The elect (detail of lintel)

Quisque resurget ita quem non trahit impia vita et lucebit ei sine fine lucerna diei
Thus shall rise again everyone who does not lead an impious life, And endless light of day shall shine for him.

4

Documentary and comparative plates

Plates a-m, *between pp. 20 and 25*; Ⓐ-Ⓐ10, Ⓑ1-Ⓑ6, *between pp. 59 and 63*; Ⓑ7-Ⓑ32, Ⓒ1-Ⓒ8, Ⓓ1-Ⓓ17, *between pp. 162 and 173*

Historical and comparative records, the tympanum and the west porch

a. View of Autun in 1591, showing St. Lazarus (top right) with the earlier cathedral of St. Nazaire to its left, and the Porte d'Arroux (foot) (From a contemporary picture of Autun under siege during the Wars of Religion, Musée Rolin, Autun)

b. The tympanum during its restoration by Viollet-le-Duc, *c.* 1858

c. The head of Christ before replacement on the tympanum in 1948

d. The tympanum in the 18th century; a contemporary model showing the plaster covering

e. The west front of St. Lazarus before rediscovery of the tympanum in 1837

f. The porch of St. Lazarus today (view from the interior) (The capitals are inspired by Roman models and may well be Roman themselves)

g. Roman capital (Musée Lapidaire, Autun) cf. the extreme left-hand capital in pl. *f*

h. Gallo-Roman pillar (Beaune Museum) cf. the trumeau and capital of the tympanum, see p. 79

i. Gallo-Roman relief of a reclining figure (Beaune Museum) cf. the *Eve* fragment from the north doorway, see p. 149

j. *Annus* holding the sun and moon (drawing of the zodiac and occupations of the months, *Chronicon Zwifaltense minus*, Stuttgart)

k. *Annus* (detail of the zodiac arch of the tympanum, Autun)

l. Seal of Étienne de Bâgé, bishop of Autun 1112-36 (Bibliothèque Nationale, Paris) cf. pl. *m*, see p. 178

m. Christ in majesty (detail of the tympanum, Autun)

The main apse and its capitals

Ⓐ View of the apse today

Ⓐ1-Ⓐ4 Lower-level capitals, not by Gislebertus: Ⓐ1 *Ira* Ⓐ2 *Lions and human head* Ⓐ3 *Two lions* Ⓐ4 *Owl*

Ⓐ5, Ⓐ6 Upper-level capitals, by Gislebertus: Ⓐ5 *Seated figure (Christ?)* Ⓐ6 *Scene with an angel*

Ⓐ7 The Porte d'Arroux, Autun (Roman gateway) cf. the use of fluted pilasters in St. Lazarus, pl. Ⓐ and plate facing p. 141

Ⓐ8 Cusped moulding, Autun (south arcade of the apse)

Ⓐ9 Cusped moulding, Cluny (transept)

Ⓐ10 The apse before removal of the 18th-century marble covering in 1939

Comparative plates, Autun and Moûtiers-Saint-Jean

Ⓑ1 Moûtiers-Saint-Jean: *The Journey to Emmaus*

Ⓑ2 Autun (Gislebertus): *The Journey to Emmaus*

Ⓑ3 *The Journey to Emmaus*—Christ shown as a pilgrim *(St. Albans Psalter)*

Ⓑ4 Autun (the Master of Moûtiers-Saint-Jean): *Christ Washing the Apostles' Feet*

Ⓑ5 Moûtiers-Saint-Jean: *Samson and the Lion*

Ⓑ6 Autun (the Master of Moûtiers-Saint-Jean): *Samson and the Lion*

Ⓑ7 Moûtiers-Saint-Jean: *Foliage capital*

Ⓑ8 Autun (Gislebertus): *Foliage capital* (the same capital is illustrated in pl. 60)

Note: the Moûtiers-Saint-Jean capitals are now in the Fogg Museum, Cambridge, U.S.A.

Sources and comparisons

Ⓑ9 Autun (Gislebertus): *Presentation of the Church* (The figures are probably those of Hugh II, duke of Burgundy and donor of the land on which the church was built, and Étienne de Bâgé, bishop of Autun, offering the as yet unfinished church to St. Lazarus)

Ⓑ10 Avenas, Rhône: *Presentation of the Church* (Early 12th-century altar frontal in the style of Cluny and Vézelay, showing the presentation of the completed church founded many centuries before, to the patron saint, St. Vincent, by a founder, probably Louis the Pious, d. 840)

Ⓑ11 Fragment by Gislebertus (?) cf. the figure of Duke Hugh II, pl. Ⓑ9; see p. 178

Ⓑ12 Cluny: *Faun and Three-headed Bird* (drawing by van Riesamburgh, 1814; the capital no longer exists)

Ⓑ13 Autun: *Faun* (detail of *Faun and Siren*, pl. 24)

Ⓑ14 Autun: *Three-headed Bird*

Ⓑ15 Vézelay: *Faun, Three-headed Bird and Siren* (capital of the main doorway)

Ⓑ16 Perrecy-les-Forges: *Faun and Three-headed Bird* (capital of the main doorway)

Ⓑ17 Cluny: *The Fourth Tone of Music*

Ⓑ18 Autun: *The Fourth Tone of Music*

Ⓑ19 Venus, Cupid and Vulcan *(Liber ymaginum deorum)* cf. the figures on the *Luxuria* capital, pl. Ⓑ20

Ⓑ20 Autun: *Luxuria*

The early career of Gislebertus

Ⓑ21 Cluny (Gislebertus?): Head of an elder of the Apocalypse (fragment from the main doorway)

Ⓑ22 Autun (Gislebertus): Head of an apostle (detail of the tympanum)

Ⓑ23 Cluny (Gislebertus?): Head (fragment from the main doorway)

Ⓑ24 Autun (Gislebertus): Head of Eve (fragment of the lintel of the north doorway)

Ⓑ25 Cluny: fragment of the mandorla (tympanum)

Ⓑ26 Autun: detail of the mandorla (tympanum)

Ⓑ27 Vézelay (Gislebertus?): mutilated tympanum of the narthex

Ⓑ28 Detail of drapery, pl. Ⓑ27

Ⓑ29 Vézelay (Gislebertus): fragment of triangular gable, *c.* 1120

Ⓑ30 Autun (Gislebertus): detail of capital, pl. 22

Ⓑ31 Vézelay (Gislebertus): fragment

Ⓑ32 Autun (Gislebertus): detail of capital, pl. 12

The style of Gislebertus: comparative details from the tympanum (including the lintel and zodiac arch), capitals and north doorway

Ⓒ1 Gestures Ⓒ2 Heads Ⓒ3 Headgear Ⓒ4 Plumage
Ⓒ5 Weave of cloth Ⓒ6 and Ⓒ7 Fringe motif Ⓒ8 Wings

The influence of Gislebertus: Beaune, La Rochepot, Saulieu, and the Ile-de-France

Ⓓ1 Beaune: *The Stoning of St. Stephen* (cf. pl. 25)

Ⓓ2 Beaune: *Noah's Ark* (cf. pl. 20)

Ⓓ3 Beaune: *The Tree of Jesse* (cf. pl. 15)

Ⓓ4 La Rochepot: *Balaam* (cf. pl. 49)

Ⓓ5 *Balaam* (*Octateuch*, Vatican, Cod. Gr. 746)

Ⓓ6 Saulieu: *Balaam* (cf. pl. 49)

Ⓓ7 Saulieu: *The First Temptation of Christ* (cf. pl. 3)

Ⓓ8 Saulieu: *Christ's Appearance to St. Mary Magdalen* (cf. pl. 21)

Ⓓ9 Saulieu: *The Suicide of Judas* (cf. pl. 17)

Ⓓ10 Saulieu: *The Flight into Egypt* (cf. pl. 5)

Ⓓ11 Saulieu: *Cockfight* (cf. pl. 23)

Ⓓ12 Saulieu: *Confronted Lions* (cf. pl. 45)

Ⓓ13 Carrières-Saint-Denis: *The Annunciation*

Ⓓ14 Autun: *The Annunciation to St. Anne*

Ⓓ15 Autun (school of Gislebertus): *Virgin and Child*

Ⓓ16 Autun (tympanum): *The Virgin Enthroned*

Ⓓ17 Carrières-Saint-Denis: *Virgin and Child*

Note: The Carrières-Saint-Denis relief (pls. Ⓓ13 and 17) is now in the Louvre, and the wooden statue of the school of Gislebertus (pl. Ⓓ15) in the Metropolitan Museum of Art, New York.

The damned (detail of lintel)

Terreat hic terror quos terreus alligat error nam fore sic verum notat hic horror specierum

Here let fear strike those whom earthly error binds, For their fate is shown by the horror of these figures.

Foreword

THE SCULPTURE OF GISLEBERTUS which decorates the cathedral of St. Lazarus at Autun ranks amongst the most important achievements of Romanesque art not only in France but in Europe as a whole. Yet, surprisingly, no recent survey of it, designed for the art lover as well as the specialist, has been published. There are, it is true, some learned articles on the subject, but they are scattered over many periodicals and are not always easily accessible. No book on Romanesque art would be complete without some reference to the sculpture of Autun but this is, as a rule, very general.

The only detailed study of the sculpture of Autun is found in the work of Abbé Victor Terret, *La sculpture bourguignonne aux XIIe et XIIIe siècles : Autun* (two volumes), Autun, 1925. This publication is a mine of information but unfortunately its learned author still shared the view, so prevalent in the 19th century, that all medieval sculpture had an allegorical meaning. He developed the idea, first put forward by Abbé Devoucoux in 1845, that the choice of subject and its presentation had been guided by the writings of Honorius Augustoduniensis. Because of this assumption, the sculpture at Autun was interpreted by Terret as serving one overriding idea, as being, in fact, a theological treatise in stone.

But such rigidity was foreign to the sculptors of the Romanesque period. Symbolism and allegory were frequently used by them but seldom, if ever, to the exclusion of a straightforward narrative, a humorous grotesque or a purely abstract decoration. A theologian often guided the work of a sculptor, but he was never a despot who left no room for spontaneous invention. Thus, although Terret's book is the most important publication on the sculpture of Autun, its bias makes the reading at times irritating. Nevertheless, much of the information is invaluable and our debt to it will be seen on almost every page.

Since Terret's pioneer book appeared thirty-six years ago, the study of Romanesque sculpture has made spectacular progress. Not only have a great number of scholars devoted much effort to research on individual monuments or groups of monuments, but also chance discoveries and planned excavations have brought to light new material. Burgundy is particularly fortunate, for the excavations at Cluny carried out by Professor Kenneth J. Conant have greatly added to our knowledge of this key monument of Romanesque art. The books of Dr. Joan Evans on the art of the Cluniac order have also opened new horizons. The researches of Marcel Aubert, Paul Deschamps, Charles and Raymond Oursel, Arthur Kingsley Porter, Pierre Quarré, Jean Vallery-Radot, Francis Salet and many others, have put new order into the history of Romanesque art in Burgundy.

At Autun itself, new and important discoveries were made. Several reliefs and other fragments of Gislebertus's work came to light, of which the most exciting was the discovery of the head of Christ which was restored to its rightful place on the west tympanum in 1948.

The present book is due entirely to the enthusiasm and labours of Mr. Arnold Fawcus, who, having visited Autun some twelve years ago, became so enchanted by Gislebertus's sculpture that he conceived the idea of paying homage to the artist by publishing a book about him. He has taken an active part in the preparation of the book at all stages and it was he who originated the collaboration of the two authors, one at Autun, the other in London. The latter wrote the text but the former contributed so much knowledge, advice and practical assistance, that the book is in fact their common effort. The London author had much further help from a number of friends and colleagues. He wishes to express his gratitude to them all, especially to Professor Jean Bony, Dr. C. R. Dodwell, M. Christopher Hohler, Mr. Peter Lasko, Mr. B. Narkiss and Professor Francis Wormald. His very special gratitude is due to M. Louis Grodecki who in 1960 gave up part of his holiday to read the text of the French edition of this book, making many invaluable corrections and suggestions. Both the authors and the publishers wish to thank the President of Magdalen for writing the introduction and reading the English text, and M. Franceschi for the great pains he took in the long work of photographing the sculptures.

DENIS GRIVOT
GEORGE ZARNECKI

he damned (detail of lintel)

Terreat hic terror quos terreus alligat error nam fore sic verum motat hic horror specierum
Here let fear strike those whom earthly error binds, For their fate is shown by the horror of these figures.

Introduction

MANY TO WHOM THE VISUAL ARTS are a clear and abiding stimulus find in their direct contact with the work no need for historical perspective and no curiosity about the artist who created it: others, perhaps today an increasing number, seek a deeper understanding of the creative process and, beyond the immediate aesthetic impact, look for iconographical interpretations and a complete artistic personality, greater in its scope than one work can by itself reveal. To the former class the admirable photographs of this volume will provide ample pleasures, different in nature from the contemplation of the sculptures themselves, for these well lit details are the product of pondered selection and emphasis, satisfying examples of interpretative skill in their own photographic right. To the second, the seekers after comprehension, the authors, the Abbé Grivot and Dr. Zarnecki, the first long familiar with the work described, the second a well known exponent of the merits of Romanesque sculpture, offer the fullest study of the creative genius of a 12th-century sculptor that has as yet been published. Gislebertus of Autun, by signing his name, GISLEBERTUS HOC FECIT, beneath the feet of Christ on the great tympanum, emerges from the anonymity of most medieval craftsmen.

In this new and very original analysis of his work he emerges also from the corporate character of the medieval mason's yard. At Vézelay M. Francis Salet has distinguished the hands of nine different sculptors, and, with whatever ingenuity such distinctions are drawn, there remains a considerable margin of carving where the attributions can only be indeterminately made. Autun has always been recognised as surprisingly uniform in its decoration. In 1939, the 18th-century marble covering of the apse was removed. On the evidence revealed, the Abbé Grivot and Dr. Zarnecki have established that there was a clear break in the type of capitals and mouldings employed, and that the predominant style first appears in the capitals of the third storey of the apse, a building stage which they date with some cogency to *c.* 1125. The key piece that proves this theory, the capital with the seated Christ, is here published for the first time. From then onwards the sculpture is marked by an individual skill and originality that belonged undoubtedly to the man whose name figures so proudly on the tympanum. Autun in comparison with Vézelay is a church of medium size. It was not impossible for one man to carve most of its decoration, and there is comparatively little indication of the assistance of pupils. It contains some ten years work by one master, and it is from this, with some backward glances at possible earlier employment, that the authors have described for us, with a consistent argument that gives a lively completeness to the subject, the progress and accomplishment of one of the great artists of the Romanesque style.

It is a style that is sympathetic to our contemporary outlook. The subject matter, the Last Judgement, scenes of the Nativity and Passion, allegories, devils, martyrdoms, belong to another way of thought, but the forms in which they were interpreted were nonnaturalistic, highly patterned and dependent for their effect on a decorative use of distortion, angularly excited poses, and variations in scale. The great semicircular bed-spread that covers the three sleeping kings is almost geometrically abstract in its curving folds, though the shy, awakening touch of the angel's hand on that of one of the sleepers is a movingly human gesture, such as is often found in the designs of Gislebertus: the angel aiding a soul to come from the tomb on the tympanum, the wonderful gesture of Christ as, on one of the capitals, he reveals himself to the Magdalen are other examples. Narrative and form meet here in a singularly happy collaboration. The angel and devil which struggle over the balance in the Judgement scene are flat, elongated, other worldly figures, as is the great central figure of Christ, but many of the smaller figures have a rounded softness which suggests actual flesh. The climax of this aspect of his work is the figure of Eve from the lintel of the north doorway. Damaged as it is, found in 1866 built into the wall of a house, it still remains one of the most sensuous of all Romanesque sculptures. Nowhere else is

Eve
(detail pl. 1)

8

the female body treated with such realism of curves or such disturbing beauty; it belongs to another age than the flatly articulated nudes of medieval manuscripts, and the haunting face, whispering through her hand to Adam, has a seductive quality that no other 12th-century artist has equalled. If the other block of the lintel, that with the similarly reclining Adam, had survived, we would almost certainly have had in it the completion of a great masterpiece. In Autun, the Augustodunum of the Romans, a *civitas* and capital of the Aedui, Roman remains were considerable: the mouldings of its still extant Roman gateway are copied in the cathedral, the pilasters are decorated with classical fluting. It is probable that some surviving classical sculpture influenced the humanist trend of Gislebertus's art.

At the opening of the 12th century Norgaud, bishop of Autun, was a resolute opponent of the Cluniac reforms, which he regarded as undermining his episcopal authority. At his death he was succeeded by Étienne de Bâgé, abbot of Saulieu, and a convinced Cluniac supporter. It is in this new atmosphere that the plans for the cathedral were undertaken, and Étienne's episcopacy, which ended in 1136, covers the main building schemes. The dukes of Burgundy were also friendly to Cluny. Hugh I retired to Cluny, where he performed the most menial offices and came to a saintly end in 1093: his brother, Odo I, campaigned against the Moors in Spain and his nephew, Hugh II (1102-1143), died returning from a pilgrimage to Compostela. A capital at Autun shows a layman and a bishop presenting the apse and transepts of a church to a figure descending from the clouds. This must represent, as the authors suggest, Hugh II, donor of the land on which the cathedral was built, and Bishop Étienne commending their church to its patron, St. Lazarus.

Cluny, Vézelay, Autun, these are the great names of Burgundian Romanesque art, as great perhaps as any that the style can claim. Cluny, centre of a great monastic reform, hub of ecclesiastical communications, for all the care that has been spent upon its ruins, remains fragmentary, though its surviving capitals of the Liberal Arts and the Rivers of Paradise have a sensitive elegance that marks a new refinement. Much of its existence is in ingenious deductions, not in actual stones and mortar. Gislebertus, our authors argue, must have been trained at Cluny, and from there went to Vézelay, where the mutilated remains of a tympanum, possibly originally designed for the main doorway, strongly suggest his handling. It is a reasonable hypothesis, supported by some further carved fragments, that when he was called to Autun, his work at Vézelay was taken over and superseded by the sculptor of the great tympanum of the west doorway, his equal, even perhaps his superior, in genius. Comparison between them is inevitable, particularly between their two tympana, closely neighbour to one another, differing in subject but each centred on the huge figure of the seated Christ. Preserved by the great narthex, unweathered by rain or wind, that of Vézelay has a sharpness of cutting that gives a liveliness and contrast to the draperies and to the attitudes of the smaller figures, whereas at Autun, protected only by an open porch, the stone has weathered, its surface is roughened and pitted, and the linear patterns faintly blurred. The tympanum at Autun, however, has fared better than Vézelay at the hands of revolutionary iconoclasts, for in 1766 it was plastered over, though the carvings of the trumeau and one of the archivolts were destroyed, and the head of Christ removed. Most fortunately this last was found and replaced in 1948, bringing an entirely new forcefulness to the whole design for it has a majestic serenity well suited to its central place, whereas formerly the blank of its absence drew the eye and disturbed the mind. Some few heads have been broken off, many to provide smoothness in the plastered surface, notably the flying angel supporting the mandorla at Christ's left hand, which must have been a charming invention; but compared with the wholesale decapitations of Vézelay, Autun is wonderfully perfect, one of the most complete of medieval survivals.

The years when Gislebertus was working at Autun were approximately 1125 to 1135. In English work of this period there is nothing that can rival the sculptural splendours of Autun and the Cluniac school of which it forms part. The capitals of the crypt at Canterbury are imaginative and accomplished decoration, but they lack the human touch, the subtleties of emotional overtones that distinguish their Burgundian contemporary. The

The Flight into Egypt
(detail pl. 5)

Chichester reliefs come much closer in feeling and execution to the style of Gislebertus, but they have a vigorous crudeness in the expressions which belongs to a more primitive tradition. The masons of Reading and of Herefordshire have a barbaric exuberance, which at Autun has been finally discarded. It is in manuscript illustration that English comparisons can be more readily found, and the capitals at Autun constantly recall the inventions and insights of the *St. Albans Psalter*, almost certainly the greatest English product in the visual arts of the 1120's, though here too the suavity of Gislebertus makes the *St. Albans* work at times seem coarse and brutal; and the Eve of the *St. Albans* Temptation is mere schematic nudity beside the rounded form of the *Eve* of Autun.

Iconographically the Autun sculptures deal with themes familiar in the Middle Ages. The Rivers of Paradise, the four musical tones, and the virtues and vices were subjects that had already been treated at Cluny. The Old and New Testament scenes are normal enough in their selection. The Last Judgement was an approved subject for the western doorway, much more conventional than the descent of the Spirit and the apostolic mission as displayed at Vézelay. No doubt the Autun programme represents clerical dictation rather than free choice on the part of the artist, but the treatment is full of originality in the details, and this certainly is contributed by Gislebertus. The famous gripping hands that close in upon the neck of the sinner have a nightmare quality that any artist of Romantic as opposed to Romanesque horror might envy. St. Peter, chained by his neck and feet, listens to the rescuing angel with a wonderfully realised intensity. The falling Simon Magus, with his hideous, lolling tongue, passes beyond the grotesque into the fearful. In the *Assumption of the Virgin*, a relief from the north doorway, we have a unique version of this theme, showing the Virgin aided from the tomb by angels, a corporeal resurrection such as was to become more fully accepted as the century progressed: the scene as designed by Gislebertus established no iconographical tradition, and remains an experimental rendering of a subject that had not yet reached a stereotyped formula.

The nearest counterparts to Autun are to be found at the churches of St. Andoche at Saulieu and of Moûtiers-Saint-Jean. The carvings of the former have always been held to precede those at Autun on the grounds that a consecration ceremony took place at Saulieu in 1119. This however, as the Abbé Grivot and Dr. Zarnecki point out, may have applied only to the transference of certain relics to the crypt and need not imply the completion of the church. Medieval consecrations are notoriously uncertain evidence for building activities. In our own time we are familiar enough with the opportunities of royal or other distinguished visits serving the occasion of foundation stone laying or formal openings somewhat out of step with the actual operations. Certainly the Saulieu capitals have all the appearance of copies and are much more easily placed as the work of an assistant of Gislebertus, re-using some of his master's designs. The Moûtiers-Saint-Jean capitals, now in the Fogg Museum at Harvard University, are by a sculptor, specimens of whose work have been found by the authors at Autun in the few capitals not from Gislebertus's own hand. These Moûtiers capitals have always been considered among the most important examples of Romanesque art available for the public of the United States. They now gain a new significance from this accurate placing of them in the complex of Burgundian art.

Here then is a book with wide implications: but the outstanding benefit it confers is the possibility of acquaintance with and understanding of a great medieval artist. As the authors analyse and document his work, one is reminded of another great piece of detection, when M. Paul Deschamps traced a 12th-century carver from a capital at Plaimpied near Bourges to the series of capitals at Nazareth, one of the crowning points of Romanesque achievement, worthy to stand beside the masterpieces of Autun. The Nazareth master remains, however, anonymous, and his peregrinations from France to Palestine a matter of speculation only. Gislebertus has now both a name and a coherent career, and worthily takes his place, a knowable personality, in the long tradition of European sculpture. As a contribution to art history, and also as a demonstration of method, this account of him will be found as fascinating to the general reader as it is impressive to the specialist.

T. S. R. BOASE

Gislebertus hoc fecit

GISLEBERTUS HOC FECIT: this inscription in the centre of the Last Judgement scene on the west tympanum of the cathedral of St. Lazarus at Autun is one of the first things that strike the visitor's eye as he approaches the main entrance. It is the signature of the artist who was responsible not only for the tympanum but also for almost all the rest of the sculptural decoration of the church.

Signatures of this kind were not unusual in the Romanesque period. What is surprising about this one is its position and importance. Earlier examples in France are found placed unobtrusively either at the base of a column (as in the crypt of St. Philibert at Tournus—RENCO ME FECIT), or more frequently on a capital (as at Bernay—ME FECIT ISEMBARDUS, and St. Benoît-sur-Loire—UNBERTUS ME FECIT). But signatures on tympana in France are very rare indeed.

As the inscription is directly beneath the feet of Christ, it might be thought its position was intended as an act of homage to God. But in inscribing his name in the most prominent place in the church, Gislebertus must have been inspired at least as much by pride in his own achievement.

This is quite consistent with what we know of the new self-confident spirit of the age, in which, long before the Renaissance, the artist claimed for himself the right of special recognition. A striving for fame was fairly general in the 12th century and at times even took the form of an almost naïve boastfulness.[1] No doubt it was the conscious imitation of the antique during this period that helped to stimulate the artist's desire for personal glory. In this context, it is interesting to observe that another French tympanum, at St. Ursin in Bourges, which is signed by one Girauldus, is decorated with subjects drawn from classical literature and art.

The church of St. Lazarus was built by the bishop and chapter of Autun, and Gislebertus's name could not have been placed where it was without their consent. We can assume from this that Gislebertus was already well-known and held in high esteem, and that in allowing his signature to be inscribed on the tympanum the bishop and canons wished it to be known that the church was decorated by no less a man than Gislebertus.

Unfortunately, there are no contemporary records to tell us anything about either Gislebertus or his work. As a result of changes in taste, his sculpture was for many years neglected and some of it even wantonly destroyed: the great west tympanum was covered with stucco for nearly a century and *Eve* served her turn as a building block in a private house. It is only in comparatively recent times that the true beauty of Gislebertus's work has been appreciated anew.

In the absence of any written records, it seems at first sight a hopeless task to attempt a critical study of Gislebertus, the artist. For at the outset we are faced with a series of problems. What were his training and previous experience? What were the sources he used, the dates of his work at Autun, his methods and aims? However, by examining his work in detail and comparing it with other sculpture in Burgundy, and by piecing together such evidence of his artistic career as does exist, many of the answers to these questions will present themselves, and we shall be able to reconstruct a fairly full picture of this astonishing artist. Before long, we shall begin to realize that in the marvellously rich field of Romanesque sculpture in France, Gislebertus holds a unique place. *He was, in fact, the only artist whose work survives, who carried out a lavish sculptural decoration of a large church practically alone during at least ten years of continuous work.*

It could be claimed that a similar situation existed elsewhere, for instance, at St. Sernin in Toulouse. But there, although we find successive stages of artistic development, it is

---

[1] As in the case, for instance, of Gilabertus of Toulouse, who signed his work: 'Vir non incertus me celavit Gilabertus' (Gilabertus who is not unknown created me), or of Eadwine, a scribe of Canterbury, who stated that his book (the *Eadwine Psalter* in Trinity College, Cambridge, MS. R. 17.1) would rightly procure him eternal fame (C. R. Dodwell, *The Canterbury School of Illumination 1066-1200*, Cambridge, 1954, p. 36).

unlikely that they represent the development of one artist. On the contrary, it is much more probable that this sculpture, as at Cluny and Vézelay, was executed by a fairly large team of very talented sculptors. In contrast, the sculpture of Autun stands out as the achievement of one man alone.

In our study of Gislebertus's art, we shall be helped by the important new material which came to light in 1939 and which has not yet been seriously discussed. In that year, the removal of the 18th-century casing of the interior of the apse revealed unexpected evidence of sculpture executed by a predecessor of Gislebertus, as well as the earliest capitals by Gislebertus himself.

Starting from this point, we shall be able to watch the work of the master step by step throughout the church, as his sculpture kept pace with the building of the cathedral, from the apse in the east to the west front. We shall be able to demonstrate that the doorway of the north transept was carved before the nave was started, and that the last and crowning achievement of the artist was the tympanum carved above the west doorway, with its monumental representation of the Last Judgement.

Our knowledge of Romanesque sculpture rests on imperfect evidence, for it is largely based on surviving monuments of a provincial nature. The great churches, the abbeys and the cathedrals had more means at their disposal of satisfying the changing tastes of subsequent generations by rebuilding the old structures, while village churches, once built, were seldom altered. The church of St. Lazarus at Autun was built neither as a cathedral nor as an abbey. In fact, its very origin is something of a mystery, for it was erected by the bishop and chapter beside an already-existing cathedral, and it was some time before it was raised to the dignity of a cathedral. However, in scale and magnificence, it was from the start designed like any abbey or cathedral, and its survival is therefore particularly fortunate. From the point of view of the history of both architecture and sculpture, it is a monument of the highest class. In Burgundy it had only two rivals: the abbeys of Cluny and Vézelay. But the first having been largely destroyed, Autun is today, together with Vézelay, the key monument of the Duchy. From the point of view of sculpture, Vézelay's title to fame is based on its superb tympanum. The rest of the decoration is of a very mixed character, executed by many sculptors, and includes works that are quite mediocre.

Autun, on the other hand, is unique in the high quality of the sculpture throughout the building. Only in the dimly-lit upper part of the building did Gislebertus allow some of his assistants to try their skill on capitals of secondary importance. Among the sculptures easily visible from the ground, there are only two capitals (both on the same pillar) that are clearly the work of another artist. It is easy to imagine an illness or some other cause which prevented Gislebertus from carving these capitals at the moment they were required.

The striking uniformity of style seen throughout the approximately ten years of Gislebertus's work at Autun does not mean that his art was static. It is true that a detailed study of his sculpture reveals that Gislebertus was fond of certain formal conventions which he used repeatedly, but in the course of time his sculpture became bolder, both technically and in its general conception.

Every artist, to be appreciated adequately, must be judged against the background of his times. For this reason, it is of great importance to discover the precise dates of the artistic activity of Gislebertus. Only then shall we be able to relate his work to the achievements of his predecessors and contemporaries, and to assess his place in the general development of Romanesque sculpture. But since, as we have said, there are no documents which can help in this respect, any dates that can be established for Gislebertus's work at Autun must be based on circumstantial evidence. We shall begin our study, therefore, with the early history of St. Lazarus, and an examination of the church that provides the setting for Gislebertus's sculpture.

St. Lazarus of Autun

CHAPTER 1

The cathedral of St. Lazarus at Autun

THE FIRST DOCUMENT referring to the church of St. Lazarus dates from 1130, when, on the 28th December, it was consecrated by Pope Innocent II.[1] St. Lazarus was built a very short distance to the south of an existing cathedral dedicated to St. Nazaire, only a few traces of which still remain. The foundation of an important new church in these circumstances seems unprecedented and the reasons for it are obscure.

Among the most treasured possessions of the cathedral of St. Nazaire were the relics of St. Lazarus, whose body rested in a sarcophagus to the right of the high altar.[2] Lazarus, *amicus Christi*, whom Christ raised from the dead and about whose subsequent history the Gospels are silent, was venerated in medieval times as a saint. It was the belief of the Greek Church that after his resurrection, Lazarus was cast adrift by the Jews in a leaky boat in the hope that he would perish at sea. However, the boat sailed all the way from Jaffa to Cyprus and Lazarus eventually became the first bishop of Kition (Larnaca); he lived on the island for more than thirty years and was buried there. His tomb was miraculously discovered in 899 and by order of the Emperor Leo VI his body was brought to Constantinople. At the same time, the body of Lazarus's sister, Mary Magdalen, was discovered in Ephesus and was also transferred to Constantinople.[3]

In the West at some later date, a legend was born, no doubt inspired by that of the Greek Church, according to which Lazarus, with his sisters Mary Magdalen and Martha, came to Gaul by sea from Palestine and became the first bishop of Marseilles. He was believed to have been buried, together with both his sisters, in Provence.[4]

Scholars are not unanimous about the origins of the cult of St. Lazarus in Burgundy.[5] The problem is certainly a complicated one and closely linked with the parallel cult of St. Mary Magdalen in the Cluniac Abbey at Vézelay. Once this was established at Vézelay, by about 1050, it seems probable that it led naturally to the cult of St. Mary Magdalen's brother, Lazarus, both at Vézelay itself and in the churches connected with it. One of these churches was at Avallon, which, although the property of the bishops of Autun, was illegally given in 1078 by Hugh I, duke of Burgundy, to Cluny. Significantly, it was during this Cluniac rule in Avallon that to the old dedication of the Virgin Mary a new one was added, namely that of St. Lazarus. At that time, a gold reliquary containing the head of St. Lazarus duly made its appearance at Avallon.

The bishop and canons of Autun regained possession of their church at Avallon in 1116,[6] and it is often asserted that only then did they claim to have in their cathedral at Autun the whole body of St. Lazarus. This, however, is clearly wrong, for it has been proved that St. Lazarus was venerated at Autun as early as the 10th century,[7] long before the cult of St. Mary Magdalen was born at Vézelay or that of St. Lazarus at Avallon. It is true that the monks of Vézelay were more successful than the canons of Autun, for their abbey became, by the end of the 11th century, one of the most important centres of pilgrimage in the whole of France.

St. Lazarus, perhaps because he was sometimes confused with the poor Lazarus of the parable, whose sores were licked by dogs,[8] became the patron of lepers, and pilgrimages to his tomb at Autun were undertaken chiefly by lepers, at that time fairly numerous in France, in the hope of a cure.[9] The lepers gathered at Autun on the 1st September, in particular, which was the day celebrated in Burgundy as the feast of the martyrdom of St. Lazarus.[10]

It was perhaps the special character of these pilgrimages that prompted the bishop and the chapter of St. Nazaire to build a separate church to which the pilgrims could be diverted. Even in the new church their presence became an embarassment and the chapter eventually built for them a vast porch which formed, so to speak, an external church where the unfortunate lepers could

---

[1] '. . . ecclesiam que in honore beati martyris dedicata et consecrata per manum domini Innocentii, apostolicae sedis ministri fuerat.' V. Mortet and P. Deschamps, *Recueil de textes relatifs à l'histoire de l'architecture*, Paris, 1929, vol. II, p. 68; C. Boëll, *Le couronnement d'Innocent II à Autun et la consécration de l'église Saint-Ladre en 1130*, in *Mémoires de la Société Éduenne*, nouv. série, t. 47, 1935, p. 126.

[2] Gagnare, *Histoire de l'église d'Autun*, Autun, 1774, p. 326.

[3] L. Duchesne, *Fastes épiscopaux de l'ancienne Gaule*, Paris, 1907, vol. I, pp. 325-6.

Until a few years ago the picturesque festival of St. Lazarus was held in Larnaca each year on the Sunday before Palm Sunday. Sir Harry Luke records (in *Cyprus*, London, 1957, p. 27) a ceremony in which a boy impersonating the saint would simulate his death and resurrection. I owe to Mrs. Charles Robertson information which was supplied by Archbishop Makarios. According to it, until recently during the week before Easter, small boys in the villages of Cyprus used to go from house to house reciting poems or telling stories about Lazarus. They were given eggs and honey afterwards. The Archbishop remembers taking part himself in these festivities. (For a description of the church and the sarcophagus of St. Lazarus at Larnaca see R. Gunnis, *Historic Cyprus*, London, 1936, p. 108.)

[4] V. Saxer, *Le culte de Marie-Madeleine en Occident*, Auxerre-Paris, 1959, vol. I, pp. 6 *seq*.

[5] The most recent study of the problem is by R. Louis, *Girart, Comte de Vienne (819-877) et ses fondations monastiques*, Auxerre, 1946.

[6] A. de Charmasse, *Cartulaire de l'église d'Autun*, Paris-Autun, 1865, pp. 4-5.

[7] P. de Vrégille, *Saint-Lazare d'Autun ou la Madeleine de Vézelay ? Un problème d'antériorité*, in *Annales de Bourgogne*, vol. XXI, 1949, pp. 34-43; also B. de Gaiffier, *Hagiographie bourguignonne*, in *Analecta Bollandiana*, vol. LXIX, 1951, p. 138.

[8] *Luke*, XVI, 19-31.

[9] Faillon, *Monuments inédits sur l'apostolat de sainte Marie-Madeleine en Provence*, Paris, 1848, t. I, p. 1189.

[10] *ibid.*, p. 1192. Certain legends claimed that St. Lazarus had suffered a martyr's death. See, for instance, the martyrology quoted by Gagnare, *op. cit.*, p. 324.

The interior of the cathedral, the south aisle

venerate the saint under cover, without entering the building itself.[1]

The cathedral of St. Nazaire stood in the upper town, close to, and within the walls of the castle, which was given by Charles the Bald to Bishop Adalgarius in about 875. Part of the castle eventually passed into the possession of the dukes of Burgundy,[2] and when the decision to build the new church close to the cathedral and within the walls of the castle was taken, the site for this enterprise was given by Duke Hugh II.[3] If the date of that gift were known, it would be possible to say with some certainty when the building of the church of St. Lazarus was begun. But although the precise date is unknown, it can be deduced with some accuracy.

The new church was consecrated in 1130 by Pope Innocent II. This does not mean that the church was finished by then. We know, in fact, that it was not even entirely ready as late as 1146.[4] The consecration of 1130 simply means that because the Pope happened to be in Autun at that time, the consecration was performed to give the ceremony greater solemnity.

Such consecrations were sometimes held over the site or over the assembled building materials even before the construction of a church had started,[5] so for our purposes the date 1130 is not a conclusive help. In a way, it is more significant that no consecration took place during the stay of Pope Calixtus II at Autun in 1119. Had the building been started at that time, the Pope would no doubt have been asked to consecrate it.

Most writers suggest that work on the church of St. Lazarus was begun about 1120,[6] and this date seems very probable indeed. The new church was the property of the bishop and the chapter of St. Nazaire but was built on a site given by Duke Hugh II. This means that the churchmen and the Duke must have been on fairly good terms. The relations between the earlier dukes of Burgundy and the bishops of Autun were notoriously bad and they improved only when in 1112 Étienne de Bâgé (de Balgiaco) was elected as bishop.[7] Within a year of assuming office, Étienne obtained from Duke Hugh II a restitution of church possessions appropriated by the duke's father.[8] Some of the promises remained

at first only on paper but by 1120 the restitution was complete.[9]

Bishop Étienne was clearly an excellent negotiator and administrator; he was also an energetic builder of churches in his diocese, a writer of distinction and a deeply religious man who finally gave up his high office in 1136 to become a monk at Cluny, where he died four years later.[10] After the turbulent career of his predecessor Bishop Norgaud, who seems to have been in conflict with everybody, Étienne established cordial relations with Cluny and the Duke, thus creating suitable conditions for such a great enterprise as the building of St. Lazarus.

It has been frequently suggested that the stay of Pope Calixtus II in Autun during Christmas 1119 probably influenced the decision to build a new church for housing the relics of St. Lazarus.[11] The Pope was related to the dukes, and his sister Ermentrude, widow of Thierry de Montbéliard, count of Bar, lived at Autun with her son Étienne, who was a canon there. There is a possibility that the Pope's visit led to a definite decision to go ahead with the building of the new church and that his sister played a prominent part in bringing the parties concerned together. She must have been a greatly honoured person, since the tomb in which she was buried with her husband was placed in the middle of the choir of St. Lazarus, until it was moved elsewhere and finally destroyed.[12] The good relations between the ducal house and the chapter of Autun lasted for some time. The successor of Bishop Étienne was Robert, one of the sons of Hugh II, but he died a few months after having been elected. His brother Henry, an archdeacon of Autun for some years, was made bishop in 1148.[13]

Thus about 1120 everything was probably ready— the site procured, the funds collected or promised and the work put into the hands of the builders. As we shall see, the work was begun from the east but after only two storeys of the apse were completed, a change was made in the design of the building. *At the same time a new sculptor appeared on the scene—Gislebertus.*[14] The work was progressing rapidly and the visit of Innocent II to Autun in 1130 was used as a suitable occasion for the consecration of the fabric which was probably already well advanced. In 1146, though the porch of the church was not entirely finished, the relics of St. Lazarus were solemnly translated from the cathedral of St. Nazaire

[1] H. de Fontenay and A. de Charmasse, *Autun et ses monuments*, Autun, 1889, p. CLIII.

[2] J. Berthollet, *L'Évêché d'Autun*, Autun, 1947, p. 43, suggests that this was probably as a result of a bargain which Duke Robert extracted from Bishop Aganon during their meeting at Autun in 1065, when St. Hugh, abbot of Cluny, acted as mediator.

[3] 'Terram scilicet in qua beati Lazari ecclesia sita est ... immunem ab omnibus exactionibus et consuetudinibus liberam ab illustri viro Hugone Burgundiae duce vobis concessam ...' Charter of Innocent II confirming the possessions of the chapter of Autun in 1132 (Charmasse, *op. cit.*, p. 6).

[4] Faillon, *op. cit.*, p. 717.

[5] R. Crozet, *Étude sur les consécrations pontificales*, in *Bulletin Monumental*, vol. 104, 1946, p. 46.

[6] R. H. L. Hamann alone (*Das Lazarusgrab in Autun*, in *Marburger Jahrbuch für Kunstwissenschaft*, vols. 8 and 9, 1936, p. 311, n. 4) dates the choir of St. Lazarus to c. 1100 on stylistic grounds.

[7] E. Petit, *Histoire des Ducs de Bourgogne*, Paris, 1885, vol. I, p. 297.

[8] For Hugh II *pacificus* see J. Richard, *Les ducs de Bourgogne et la formation du duché du XIe au XIVe siècle*, Paris, 1954, p. 150.

[9] It was only then that the duke agreed to the return of Avallon (Louis, *op. cit.*, p. 179).

[10] For his *Tractatus de Sacramento Altaris*, see Migne, *Patrol. Lat.*, Paris, vol. 172, 1854, col. 1274 *seq.*

[11] A view already expressed by Abbé Devoucoux (*Description de l'église cathédrale d'Autun par un chanoine de cette église*, Autun, 1845, p. 6).

[12] Gagnare, *op. cit.*, p. 330.

[13] U. Plancher, *Histoire générale et particulière de Bourgogne*, Dijon, 1739, vol. I, p. 298. The suggestion of Gagnare (*op. cit.*, p. 314) that St. Lazarus was built by the dukes of Burgundy as a palace chapel (*Chapelle Palatine*) is not convincing. The dukes did not live in the castle of Autun, except on occasional visits, and none of them was buried in St. Lazarus, as would, no doubt, have been the case if it had been their palace chapel.

[14] See pp. 57-58.

to the new church dedicated to him.[1] Later in that century, during the time of Bishop Étienne II (1170-89), the relics were placed in a splendid tomb, fragments of which are preserved in the Musée Rolin at Autun.[2]

There can be no doubt that the church of St. Lazarus was not built to replace the cathedral of St. Nazaire. Throughout the 12th century, St. Nazaire alone was the cathedral of Autun, and only in 1195 did St. Lazarus become a cathedral. But even then, there was no question of abandoning the earlier building. On the contrary, in the middle of the 13th century, the rebuilding of the old cathedral was started but the project was too ambitious and was never finished. St. Nazaire fell into ruins and was eventually pulled down in the 18th century.

The other major medieval churches in Autun, including the important abbey of St. Martin, vanished too. It is particularly fortunate, therefore, that St. Lazarus has survived and is comparatively well preserved.

The cathedral of St. Lazarus is not orientated due east, as was customary, but slightly south-east. This was probably dictated by the shape of the available site within the walls of the castle, perched on top of the hill of the upper town. (See pl. *a*.)

The church is of the basilican form with a nave and aisles of seven bays (see plate facing p. 141), a transept projecting considerably beyond the aisles and a choir of two bays flanked, like the nave, by aisles and terminating in three apses. The central apse was dedicated to St. Lazarus, and the lateral apses, very appropriately, to his two sisters: the northern to St. Mary Magdalen and the southern to St. Martha.[3] In front of the central apse was the tomb containing the relics of St. Lazarus, and adjoining it, on the west side, was the high altar. In the 18th century, the tomb was broken up and sold and the interior of the central apse covered, at great expense, by a layer of marble (see pl. Ⓐ10). In the process, those capitals that projected from the wall-face were ruthlessly mutilated. In 1939, this screen of marble was removed, revealing the 12th-century masonry practically intact, and the capitals.[4] *These, although badly damaged, are of great importance as those of the upper level are the earliest surviving work of Gislebertus at Autun.*[5]

The internal elevation of the church follows closely the model set by the great abbey of Cluny built between

1086 and 1121.[6] The church is divided horizontally into three storeys, of which the lowest is twice as high as the other two combined. The ground arcade consists of pointed arches resting on massive cruciform piers. Above is the triforium with a passage over the vaulting of the aisles. Seen from the nave, this storey appears as a triple arcade within each bay, only one of the arches being open. The uppermost storey consists of a single window to each bay, whereas at Cluny there were three. The transverse ribs of the vaulting rest on capitals supported by flat, fluted pilasters which are carried down on to the piers (see plate facing p. 141 and plan VIII).

Fluted pilasters were used at Cluny a little earlier, but the motif is, of course, of classical origin. One of the Roman gateways still surviving at Autun, known as the Porte d'Arroux, must have been well-known to the builders of Romanesque churches in Burgundy, and supplies a splendid example of the use of fluted pilasters (see pl. Ⓐ7).

In the choir and transept, the arcades of the triforium are blind, for there is no triforium passage behind them. The extreme bays of the transepts consist of two arches, instead of three, and there is another irregularity in the design of the last bay on each side of the nave where all three arches are blind, instead of one being open as in the other arcades of the nave.

Throughout the church, the arcades of the triforium are separated by fluted pilasters and simple foliage capitals; this is a departure from the design used at Cluny and an indication of the direct influence of the Porte d'Arroux. There is no uniformity in the treatment of the capitals and in the last bay but one of the nave, on the south side, one capital is enriched with an interlacing motif while another is carved with an animal's head.

The whole church was vaulted, the nave, transept and choir having pointed barrel vaulting and the aisles groin vaulting, both with transverse ribs. The crossing is surmounted by a dome supported by squints: the central tower above is a work of the 15th century, replacing the original 12th-century structure.

The piers of the crossing, supporting the tower, were rebuilt and enlarged by additional masonry and angle columns during the restoration, which was begun in 1860, under the direction of Viollet-le-Duc. The capitals of these and of some of the neighbouring piers were then replaced by copies but the originals were luckily preserved and are now in the cathedral museum (see plans V and VI and fig. 5, pp. 66 *et seq.*).

The exterior of St. Lazarus gives the impression, at first sight, of a 15th-century building, so much has its original design been destroyed or obscured. The central tower, as we have already mentioned, was rebuilt in the late Gothic style after being damaged by lightning in 1469.[7]

---

[1] 'Vestibulum, quod vestire et delucidare ecclesiam debet, nondum confirmatum esse, pavimenta, ut decebat in tam nominata domo, juxta ingenium artificis, nec sculta, nec ad unguem aptata fore; adhuc innumera restare quae dignum erat in ingressu Domini domus integre consummari.' From the account of an eye-witness of the translation of the relics, the full text of which is quoted by Faillon, *op. cit.*, pp. 715-24. See also Mortet and Deschamps, *op. cit.*, p. 68.

[2] Hamann, *op. cit.*

[3] M. Pellechet, *Notes sur les livres liturgiques des diocèses d'Autun, Chalon et Mâcon*, Paris-Autun, 1883, pp. 315 and 375.

[4] M. A. Colombet, *Le dégagement et la restitution de l'ancien chœur roman de la cathédrale d'Autun*, in *Mémoires de la Commission des Antiquités du département de la Côte-d'Or*, vol. 22, 1940-41 (1948), pp. 139 seq.

[5] See pp. 57-58, pls. Ⓐ1-Ⓐ6 and 161-2.

[6] K. J. Conant, *Carolingian and Romanesque Architecture, 800-1200*, in *The Pelican History of Art*, 1959, p. 116.

[7] V. Terret, *La sculpture bourguignonne aux XIIᵉ et XIIIᵉ siècles*, Autun, Autun, 1925, vol. I, p. 33 et n. 4. (This work will be referred to from now on as: Terret, *Autun*, I or II.)

Its beautiful, graceful spire dominates the city and provides a familiar landmark.

The western porch is an impressive structure, although it has suffered greatly from rebuilding and restoration (see pls. *e* and *f*). An open porch, with a small chapel of St. Michael above it, existed when the relics of St. Lazarus were translated from St. Nazaire to the new church in 1146, though it was then unfinished.[1] At first it enclosed only the central and south entrances to the church but it was enlarged and rebuilt in 1178 to include all three doorways.[2] The porch is the same width as the church, and like it is divided by arcades into three compartments, each of which consists of two bays, corresponding with the nave and aisles. Subsequently the arcades of the aisles in the porch were blocked up and two small chapels were made. The ground in front of the central porch was used for a long time as a burial place for the clergy and the benefactors of the church.

The access to the porch was by way of steps on its north side. The burial ground was suppressed in 1767 and in 1848 a new approach to the church was made with the steps facing the main doorway. In 1855 the steps were extended across the whole width of the porch and the chapels in its aisles were therefore demolished. The original turrets of the porch were rebuilt in 1873 on the model of Paray-le-Monial.[3] The oratory of St. Michael in the top storey of the porch was a direct imitation of the corresponding chapel at Cluny built in the thickness of the wall above the central doorway and also dedicated to St. Michael.[4]

The part of the exterior of St. Lazarus which has best retained its original appearance is the north transept, where the blind arcade with fluted pilasters corresponds with the false triforium of the interior. Above, on the north wall, there are two windows with carved capitals and higher still, below the gable, a blind arcade with a large window in its centre. The blind arcade at this level of the transept joins the arcade which runs around the whole church under the eaves. The north aisle of the choir retains the only surviving section of the original corbel table.

In the centre of the north wall of the north transept is a large doorway (ruthlessly altered in the 18th century to meet contemporary tastes) which was originally facing the cathedral of St. Nazaire and provided the shortest route between the two churches. As far as can be judged, there was no corresponding doorway in the south transept.[5]

The Gothic appearance of the exterior of St. Lazarus is due also to the chapels and the flying buttresses. These last were added at the very end of the 13th century as a result of the dangerous condition of the upper walls, which the thrust of the vault was pushing out of the vertical. Thanks to this remedy, the vault survived till 1845 when it was replaced by a construction of lighter materials, preserving, however, the original form.

The chapels added to the aisles of the church on either side correspond with the seven bays of these aisles; they all date from the 15th and 16th centuries. On the south side of the choir, a sacristy was built by Cardinal Jean Rolin, bishop of Autun (1436-63); this is now converted into a chapel. A larger sacristy adjoining the south transept was built in 1520. The upper storey of this building was used originally as the Chapter Library; many of its books, including precious manuscripts, are in the Bibliothèque Municipale of Autun. The room itself, known as the 'Salle Capitulaire', is now used as the cathedral museum, and contains the capitals which were replaced by copies during the 19th century.

---

[1] Mortet and Deschamps, *op. cit.*, pp. 67-69.

[2] Terret, *Autun*, I, p. 33. The text of the act of concession passed by Duke Hugh III in relation to this porch was published by Charmasse, *op. cit.*, pp. 109-11, and by Mortet and Deschamps, *op. cit.*, vol. II, p. 133.

[3] This is the date quoted by *Congrès Archéologique de France*, 1899, p. 65. Terret (*Autun*, I, p. 33) gives the dates of the reconstruction as 1868-70.

[4] Conant, *op. cit.*, p. 119 and pl. vb. The porch at Autun was compared with that of Cluny by Jean Vallery-Radot, *Notes sur les chapelles hautes dédiées à saint Michel*, in *Bulletin Monumental*, vol. 88, 1929, p. 468.

[5] In 1520 a sacristy was built against the south transept and this structure disturbed much of the original masonry there. Consequently, it is difficult to be certain whether there was any doorway on that side of the cathedral; at any rate, if there were, it could not have been very large.

PLS. *a-m: Historical and comparative records, the tympanum and the west porch*

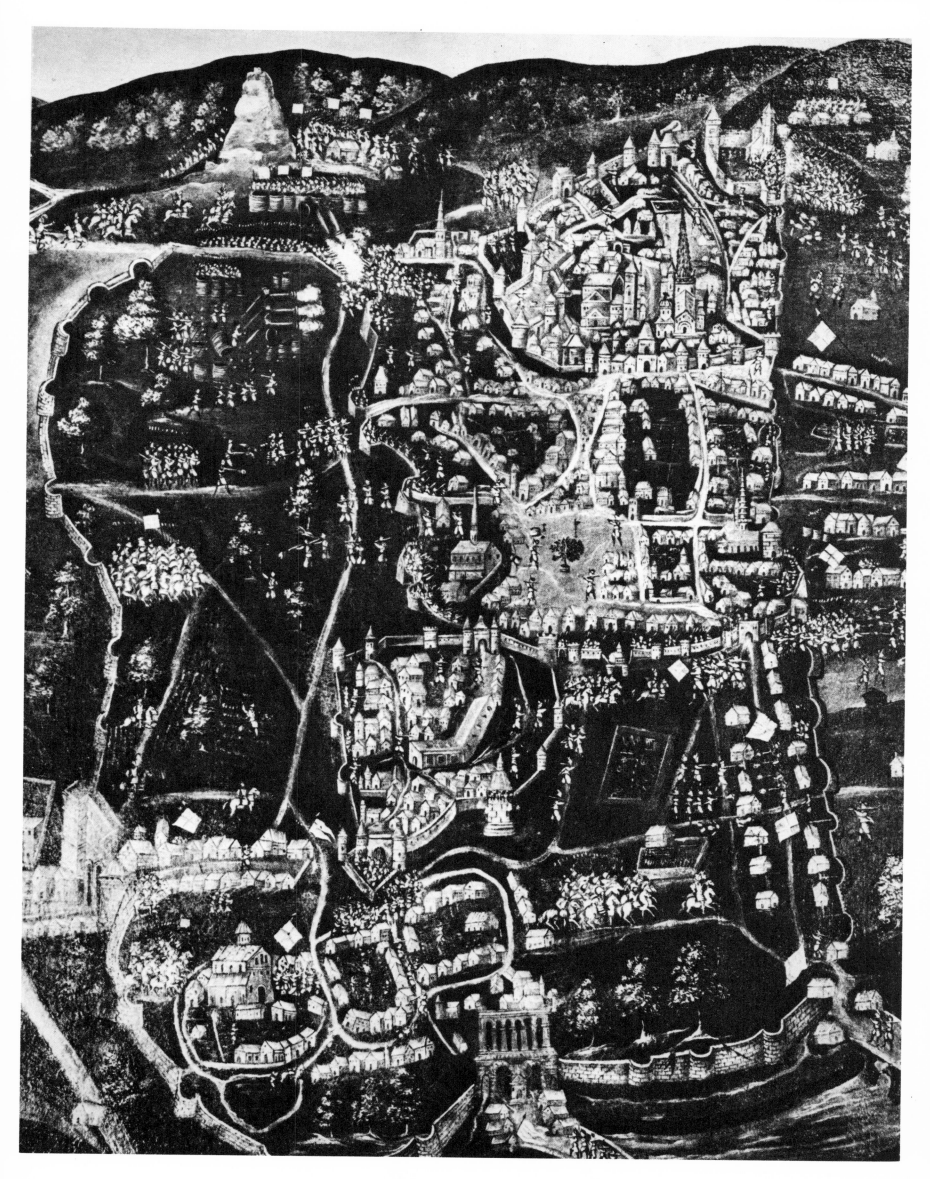

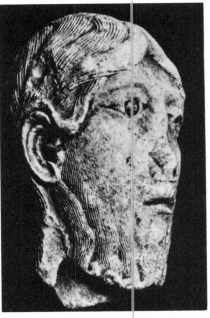

c. Head of Christ before replacement

b. The tympanum during its restoration by Viollet-le-Duc, c. 1858

e. West front of St. Lazarus before rediscovery of the tympanum in 1837

d. The tympanum in the 18th century;
a contemporary model showing the plaster covering

←— a. View of Autun in 1591,
showing St. Lazarus (top right)
and the Porte d'Arroux (foot)

g. Roman capital (Musée Lapidaire, Autun)
cf. the extreme left-hand capital in pl. f

h. Gallo-Roman pillar (Beaune Museum)
cf. tympanum trumeau and capital, see p. 79

f. The porch of St. Lazarus today (view from the interior)

i. Gallo-Roman relief of a reclining figure (Beaune Museum)
cf. the *Eve* fragment from the north doorway, see p. 149

j. Annus holding the sun and moon
(drawing of the zodiac and occupations of the months,
Chronicon Zwifaltense minus, Stuttgart)

k. Annus (detail of the zodiac arch
of the tympanum, Autun)

l. Seal of Étienne de Bâgé, bishop of Autun 1112-36

m. Christ in majesty
(detail of the tympanum, Autun)

CHAPTER 2

The doorway of the west façade and its tympanum

THE MAIN ENTRANCE to the cathedral is by a large central doorway in the west façade. This doorway incorporates an enormous tympanum made of twenty-nine pieces of stone, skilfully fitted together [pl. B; plans I and II, p. 30]. The width of the tympanum at its base is 6.40 m. and its average thickness is 35 cm. although a few of the heads project by some further 10 cm. These figures explain why, for reasons of elementary safety, it was necessary to give the tympanum the support of a lintel of sufficient solidity. The height of the lintel used for this purpose is 76.5 cm., its thickness 40 cm. and its length 6.40 m. At both ends, the lintel rests on a square capital, thus having at each extremity a support along 44 cm. of its length. The span of the lintel between these two capitals is 5.52 m., a length which it would be unsafe to leave without any additional support as the weight of the tympanum could break the lintel. For this reason, the lintel is supported in its centre by a trumeau, which divides the central doorway in two. The additional advantage of giving the lintel a central support is obvious. Instead of having to handle one enormous block of stone, the sculptor employed two pieces which were joined above the trumeau. In spite of all the precautions taken to provide adequate support for the tympanum, the lintel has cracked in two or three places.

Most of the figures carved on the tympanum are in high relief or even in the round and the average projection of the sculpture from the background is 25 cm. The figures on the lintel, which are considerably smaller, project only by some 12 cm.

To carve a tympanum of this size and thickness was an extremely difficult undertaking, and it is understandable that the sculptor preferred to employ not a monolithic block of stone but smaller, more manageable pieces, even if this method demanded fitting together and concealing, as far as possible, the joins of twenty-nine separate stones. The difficulty of his task will be appreciated if it is borne in mind that the large tympanum at Vézelay is made of only nine separate pieces of stone.[1]

The material used for the tympanum is a rather hard, whitish limestone not found in the local quarries but strongly resembling the stone quarried at Tournus and in the neighbourhood of Chalon and Beaune. The local sandstone from which St. Lazarus is built was obviously not suitable for carving and a better stone was brought for the sculptured parts of the fabric. The capitals of the main apse are made of the same limestone as the tympanum. But for the carved capitals in the rest of the church yet a different stone was used. The majority are in oolitic limestone, characterised by a rather thick grain, and resembling the limestone of the Charolais. A few capitals, now in the 'Salle Capitulaire', are made of a grained stone containing mica.[2]

The central doorway of St. Lazare has not survived the last eight hundred years without considerable damage. Of the three arches over the tympanum, one is plain, though originally it was carved.[3] Its decoration was erased in 1766 by the cathedral chapter itself. The canons, ashamed of this work of the 'age of superstition' had the figures carved on the trumeau cut away and the tympanum covered with bricks and plaster.[4] The head of Christ and the figures on the arch around the tympanum projected too much out of the alignment and were consequently broken off. At the same time both the tympanum and the trumeau of the north doorway were also destroyed. (See pls. b, c, d, e.)

The tympanum remained hidden under plaster until 1837, when a local archeologist, Abbé Devoucoux, rediscovered it. In his diary is the following entry for 23rd May: 'The report of the enquiry made in 1482[5] for the purpose of establishing the authenticity of the relics of St. Lazarus, contains a description of the church; there it states that the doorway is decorated with a relief representing the Last Judgement. Today I arranged for an examination of the plaster which was put there by architects of no taste in the last century. Fortunately, the sculpture beneath it is preserved. Mortar and plaster were merely applied over the original work which seems very accomplished for its period.'[6]

In the same diary there is a further entry on the subject, under 29th September: 'Today the workmen began to uncover the reliefs which decorate the tympanum of the church. M. Robelin, the architect from Paris, was present at this operation to ensure that it was carried out with due care.'

---

[1] F. Salet, *La Madeleine de Vézelay*, Melun, 1948, p. 142.

[2] The examination of the various stones used at Autun was carried out, at our request, by M. P. C. Fournier, the architect of the Monuments Historiques for the Saône-et-Loire. We acknowledge with gratitude his kind help.

[3] Devoucoux, *op. cit.*, p. 37.

[4] L. Réau, *Les monuments détruits de l'art français*, Paris, 1959, vol. I, p. 119. M. Réau is not aware that the figures of the arch were destroyed during this operation. This, however, is quite definitely stated by Devoucoux: 'Les débris de ces figures, détachées à l'époque des malheureuses restaurations de 1760, ont été retrouvés, mais trop mutilés pour être appliqués de nouveau' (*op. cit.*, p. 37). Devoucoux consistently speaks of the restoration of 1760 but the correct date is 1766 (see Fontenay and Charmasse, *op. cit.*, p. 416, n. 2). The relevant description in the report of 1482 is printed in our note no. 7, p. 78.

[5] The manuscript was deposited in the Musée Rolin at Autun by the Société Éduenne.

[6] The Abbé's diary is also in the Musée Rolin.

The discovery was followed by a restoration carried out by Viollet-le-Duc which started in 1860. In the course of this work, the mutilated trumeau was replaced by a modern reconstruction of the figures of Lazarus, Mary and Martha. To what extent it is based on the original it is not possible to judge, since the old trumeau was thrown away. The capital surmounting the trumeau is also modern, but in this case it is now known to be a fairly faithful copy of the original; this, though very damaged and broken into three pieces, has been preserved.[1]

A great event in the history of the tympanum was the identification of the head of the central figure of Christ, broken off in 1766, which eventually found its way into the Musée Rolin. The head was put back in place on 17th November 1948.[2]

The centre of the tympanum is occupied by a large figure of Christ, seated on a throne, with both arms outstretched. He is shown within a mandorla on which is written the following inscription:

*OMNIA DISPONO   SOLUS MERITOS[QUE] CORONO
QUOS SCELUS EXERCET   ME JUDICE POENA COERCET*

[I alone dispose of all things and crown the just,
Those who follow crime I judge and punish]

The first part of the inscription, to the right of Christ (and to the left of the onlooker) refers to everything that is depicted on that side of the tympanum and the corresponding part of the lintel. The inscription on Christ's left, which speaks of punishment, refers to practically everything on this side, with the exception of a few of the figures closest to Christ.

Me judice, says the inscription. And indeed Christ here presides over the Last Judgement. The mandorla, the sign of glory, is supported by four angels: two standing and two flying, their heads downwards. In the medallions above Christ are heads symbolising the sun and the moon. The tympanum to the right and left of Christ is divided by a horizontal arcaded projection into the upper and lower registers. At the extreme ends of each register are angels sounding long horns to announce the Last Judgement [pls. C and K, M and N].

The upper register must be intended to represent heaven for here, on the right hand of Christ, his mother sits on a throne [pl. M]. On the other side are two seated figures [pl. N], which are usually believed to be apostles, because, with the ten apostles on the lower register, they make the traditional number of twelve. The place of honour occupied by the two seated figures could have

been given only to St. Peter and St. Paul; but St. Peter, who can easily be recognised by his keys, is represented among the ten apostles standing to the right of Christ. Thus, the two seated figures are probably not apostles but perhaps Elijah and Enoch who were carried up to heaven alive. It was believed during the Middle Ages that these two would be the only people from Old Testament times who would witness the Last Judgement.[3]

Below the lower register, to the right of Christ, is the following inscription:

*QUISQUE RESURGET ITA   QUEM NON TRAHIT IMPIA VITA
ET LUCEBIT EI   SINE FINE LUCERNA DIEI*

[Thus shall rise again everyone who does not lead an
impious life,
And endless light of day shall shine for him]

This part of the tympanum and the corresponding half of the lintel show the resurrection of the elect, with St. Peter and a group of eight apostles standing in veneration.

The rest of the tympanum becomes clearer if we look first at the lintel, examining it from left to right [pls. Q and R]. On the lower edge of the lintel are carved tombs from which the dead are raised by the call of the angels' horns. In the centre, under Christ's feet, stands an angel with a sword, dividing the elect from the damned.

The elect occupy the left side of the lintel. Some are just stepping out of their sarcophagi, others stand in or on them. Three have cloaks over their shoulders; the remainder are nude with the exception of three ecclesiastics, two bishops or abbots and a monk, who are fully clothed. Two pilgrims have their staffs across their shoulders and large scrips with badges: a cross for Jerusalem and a cockle-shell for Santiago de Compostela. Two charming groups are particularly worthy of attention: an angel surrounded by three children, who cling to it as if to beg for protection [pl. A]; and nearby a man and a woman, who are clearly husband and wife: he clasps her hand while she points to their child still freeing itself from its shroud. Some of the elect already contemplate God, others show signs of excitement and joy.

The figures on the right-hand half of the lintel are the damned and the inscription below the corresponding half of the tympanum reads:

*TERREAT HIC TERROR   QUOS TERREUS ALLIGAT ERROR
NAM FORE SIC VERUM   NOTAT HIC HORROR SPECIERUM*

[Here let fear strike those whom earthly error binds,
For their fate is shown by the horror of these figures]

The damned are all shown in the nude. Some cover their faces in terror; a miser with a bag of money hanging round his neck and a snake twined round his body, is

---

[1] The three pieces dispersed in different places at Autun were identified in 1960 and are now assembled in the Musée Rolin (pls. 50*a* and *b*).

[2] As a result of its identification by Abbé Grivot and Abbé Berthollet, the head was fixed in place by the service of the Beaux-Arts (cf. *Arts*, 25th December 1949).

[3] A Priest, *The Masters of the West Façade of Chartres*, in *Art Studies*, vol. I, 1923, p. 37, identified two figures who appear with the apostles on the lintel of the central doorway at Chartres as Elijah and Enoch.

clearly screaming. An adulterous woman has two snakes biting her breasts. The figure next to her is being strangled by two enormous claw-like hands [pl. P].

The last figure but one on the right has been generally interpreted as representing Intemperance, beating his barrel of wine. It seems more likely—since the 'barrel' is actually a flat circular object decorated with a cross— that it represents a Jew, holding a Eucharistic Host and a knife. His place among the damned would be in keeping with the widespread accusations of ritual murder and sacrilegious practices levelled against Jews in the Middle Ages.

The story which is begun on the lintel is continued on the tympanum. Here, to the left of the group of apostles worshipping Christ stands the large figure of St. Peter with an enormous key to the gate of heaven [pls. D and E]. This stands open at the very top. Inside heaven, which is represented by arcades, there are already a few souls. One is being lifted up by an angel and is climbing inside [pl. C]. In contrast to the opposite side of the tympanum, here all is gentleness. The soul of a child embraces an angel; St. Peter takes another figure by the hands, while yet another soul raises itself up by holding on to one of the angels blowing a horn.

On the other side of the tympanum—the side of the damned— is the figure of a saint holding a book, probably St. John. Next to him stands the Archangel Michael, with two souls clinging to his garments and seeking protection. The Archangel is weighing souls, and has a devil as his adversary [pl. J]. The devil is made to look horrible not only by his monstrous head, tail and claws but by his thin, skinny body, half-human, half-reptile. In contrast to St. Michael whose garments serve as a refuge for souls, the devil drags an unfortunate by the hair while a three-headed snake coils between his legs. In representations of the *Psychostasis* (the weighing of souls), it is the Archangel who usually carries the scales but here they are held by a hand emerging from the clouds of heaven.[1] The soul whose destiny is at stake is clearly one of the elect, for it is being received by the Archangel, while the devil tries to tilt the balance in his favour and a smaller devil sits in the scales to counterbalance the weight of the soul. The soul of another elect is shown in mid-air obviously on its way to heaven. An even more dreadful and larger devil than the one facing St. Michael stands behind carrying a toad [pl. L]. On the extreme right of the tympanum is the gate of hell from behind which emerges the head of the Leviathan and a devil pulling a woman towards him with a curved fork [pl. K]; she is no doubt an adultress as a snake coils round her body and bites her breast. With his other hand, the same devil is hoisting up three souls chained together by their necks.

Above the gate of hell is a cauldron licked by flames. Standing with one leg half in the cauldron itself, yet another devil is about to throw two terrified souls into the fire. The feet appearing over the edge of the cauldron suggest that many of the souls of the damned have already found their way there [pl. L].

Many of the elements which form part of the Autun tympanum were traditional, taken from written and visual sources. But the whole composition as conceived by Gislebertus was new and remained unique. He was a visionary who created an image as full of drama as any in the *Book of Revelations*. Both the context and the form are charged with almost unbearable tension. The only static figure is that of Christ who dominates everything by his gigantic size and his expression of almost frightening gravity [pls. H and I]. The gesture of his arms separating the good from the evil sets the drama in motion [pls. F and G]. Even the Virgin, the prophets and the apostles express something of this mood of tension. But it is the right side of the lintel and that part of the tympanum which depicts the weighing of souls and the sufferings of the damned which brings this tension to its highest pitch. Here we can almost hear the screams of the damned, the noise of the chains and the sound of the horns. When the tympanum was painted, as it undoubtedly was, the vividness of all the details must have been even more striking.[2]

Most men in the Middle Ages were preoccupied with the terrors of hell, devils and monsters, and the artists almost delighted in giving these notions as dreadful a form as possible. Gislebertus was no exception to this. On the contrary, he even surpassed his contemporaries in some of his inventions. After seeing his work, who can forget, for instance, the expression of utter terror on the face of the figure seized by the throat by two enormous hands appearing from nowhere [pl. P], or that procession of men and women whose expressions and gestures show so vividly that there is no hope for them —only eternal despair?

Some people, even eminent scholars, have criticized the proportions of Gislebertus's figures. 'The artist, in fact, composed his tympanum so awkwardly that in order to fill in the central register he was obliged to elongate the figures out of all proportion', wrote Émile Mâle.[3] Such a view completely overlooks the fact that Romanesque artists did not attempt to imitate the precise forms found in nature but used them freely as it suited their aims. *La loi du cadre* which, according to Henri Focillon,[4] guided them consciously or unconsciously, accounts for a great many of the distortions of form dictated by the shape and nature of the material in which the sculptor worked. But these were not the only reasons for distortions. We know that, when he wished to do so, Gislebertus was quite capable of giving his figures correct

---

[1] The subject is discussed by M. P. Perry, *On the Psychostasis in Christian Art*, in the *Burlington Magazine*, 1912-13, pp. 94 and 208, and L. Kretzenbacher, *Die Seelenwaage*, Klagenfurt, 1958.

[2] It will be seen that one of the interior capitals still retains traces of the original colours. The fragments of the Cluny tympanum also bear traces of colours (see K. J. Conant, *Medieval Academy Excavations at Cluny, The Season of 1928*. Offprint from *Speculum*, vol. IV, 1929, p. 14).

[3] E. Mâle, *L'art religieux du XIIᵉ siècle en France*, Paris, 1924, p. 416.

[4] H. Focillon, *Art d'Occident*, Paris, 1938, pp. 98-105.

forms and proportions; we have numerous examples of his work to prove this. If at times, and especially in carving the tympanum, he departed in such a striking degree from nature, he clearly did so deliberately. The *Last Judgement* cannot be anything but a vision and those who take part in it are not human beings but saints, angels, resurrected souls and demons. Gislebertus conceived his vision in supernatural, not human, terms. This is why Christ dominates and overshadows the whole composition, for it is he who conditions everything. Compared with him, everything is on a totally different scale. Some of the apostles nearest to Christ appear to grow in size by virtue of their closeness to him. It would have been easy for Gislebertus to divide the tympanum into tidy registers and place the figures of equal size within them. But he clearly did not seek such a solution. The varying sizes of the figures, their very elongation, give the tympanum its unique impression of the supernatural.

The emotional tension is achieved not only by the expressions and gestures of those taking part in this drama, but also by plastic and compositional means. The folds of the robes, with their unexpected twists and curling hems, the placing of figures or their grouping, some facing the central figure of Christ, in other cases turning away from him, the grouping of large numbers of figures closely set together while others stand out isolated against a flat background, are only some instances of this.

Not only is the Autun tympanum a supreme work of art, but it is also a masterpiece from a purely technical point of view. The ease with which the sculptor carved his figures in bold relief, some almost in the round, with only a few blocks joining them to the background, is really amazing if we think of the modesty and hesitation of the sculptors of the previous generation.

The immediate successors of the Autun *Last Judgement* show the rapidly changing taste of the age. The dramatic and narrative elements, still present at Conques and Beaulieu and even St. Denis, were replaced at Chartres, and in works inspired by it, by more static and intellectual compositions. But the dramatic vision of Gislebertus was reintroduced again in a modified form in the tympana of the 13th century.

The founders of the cathedral clearly appreciated the quality of Gislebertus's tympanum and the renown which it would bring to the church, since they arranged for, or at least permitted, the signature of the artist to be inscribed in the centre of the tympanum under Christ's feet—*Gislebertus hoc fecit.*

The arches

The tympanum is encircled by three arches, each of which rests on a pair of capitals and columns [pl. B]. In addition, there is an outer hood enriched with a beaded ornament.

The outermost arch is carved with thirty complete medallions and one half medallion, which is on the extreme right [pls. O1-31]. A careful examination of the decoration of this arch reveals that it must have been carved in the workshop *before* being set up in position. A similar method was probably used for all the sculptural decoration of Autun. It is very likely that, when the medallions were first drawn with a compass, there were thirty-one of them. The carving was no doubt started from the left end of the arch and proceeded clockwise. The distances between the medallions are very small, but they vary slightly and it was probably the occasional increase in the distance between some of the medallions that resulted in the final miscalculation: by the time the right end of the arch was reached, there was room for only a half medallion.

It is interesting to compare this Autun arch with the corresponding arch around the central tympanum at Vézelay. There, the carving was done *in situ*[1] and the sculpture was clearly started simultaneously from both ends. By the time the top of the arch was reached, a small miscalculation was discovered and this was over-come by making one of the medallions oval instead of circular.[2]

The manner in which the subjects are carved within the medallions at Autun and Vézelay supplies further proof that a different procedure of carving was adopted in each case. At Vézelay, where the arch was already set up in its present position before the carving was started, the sculptor was standing on a scaffolding, and he consequently placed the figures vertically, for that was the most convenient way of carving them. At Autun, on the other hand, the position of the figures within the medallions varies from one to another. Carving on the bench of the workshop, Gislebertus made no allowance for the point of view of the future spectator and consequently some of the figures appear horizontal while others are vertical or diagonal.

Except for two purely decorative medallions on the left, and one and a half on the right, all the subjects are illustrations of the calendar. The idea was to relate the annual movement of the sun through the twelve constellations of the zodiac, to man's activities. The origin of these representations goes back to classical times, but it was only in the 12th century that the calendar was used to decorate the doorways of churches. By far the greatest number of such decorations are found in France.[3]

---

[1] Salet, *op. cit.*, pp. 143-4.

[2] *ibid.*, pl. 16a.

[3] J. C. Webster, *The Labors of the Months in Antique and Medieval Art*, Princeton, 1938, p. 78.

At Autun, the cycle consists not only of the usual twelve signs of the zodiac and the related occupations of each of the twelve months, but there are also three additional medallions, the subjects of which can be identified with the help of an illuminated manuscript. This manuscript is the *Chronicon Zwifaltense minus* at Stuttgart[1] which has on folio 6 v⁰ a drawing showing the signs of the zodiac and the occupations of the months arranged in two circles [pl. *j*]. In the centre is a crouching figure symbolising the year and inscribed *Annus*. In the four corners of this drawing are representations of the four seasons, also identified by inscriptions. Thus Spring is shown as a youth in a short tunic who carries branches or flowers. Summer is represented as a nude figure with a sickle, Autumn carries fruit while Winter is a man in a tunic and coat, with a hood on his head, warming himself in front of a fire. Outside the margin of this illumination are four figures symbolising Morning, Noon, Evening and Night.

At Autun, the first two figural medallions (starting from the left) preceding the calendar, represent the four seasons, arranged in two pairs.[2] The seasons are shown as young men, each differently dressed. In the first medallion is Spring, in a short tunic and holding some branches or flowers; the other figure is Autumn, dressed in a tunic and a cloak which gives the impression of being blown by the wind. The other pair clearly consists of Winter dressed in a thick coat with a hood but without sleeves, and Summer, a nude figure with a cloak thrown over one shoulder, while the face is covered by one hand as if to provide shade from the sun.

The similarity in the treatment of the seasons in the Stuttgart manuscript and the Autun medallions leaves no room for doubt that the identification of the subjects is correct. Medallion No. 15, which is almost at the apex of the arch, is carved with a crouching figure in which Abbé Terret saw the solstice of the summer.[3] Such an identification, though certainly ingenious, cannot be supported by any contemporary analogies. The crouching figure representing the Year in the Stuttgart manuscript bears, however, a sufficient resemblance to the Autun carving to justify a similar identification.

In the Stuttgart manuscript, *Annus* is shown holding in each hand a medallion on which the sun and moon are represented each by a human face. At the top of the Autun tympanum, above Christ and his mandorla, one can see symbols of exactly the same kind—indicating how much fuller is the cosmology illustrated at Autun than might be thought at first glance.

The calendar representations begin immediately after the seasons on the fifth medallion [pls. O5 *et seq.*] and are as follows:

5. *January:* Feasting. A man warmly dressed and seated in front of a fire is about to cut a cake or bread with a large knife. At Vézelay, January is an almost exact replica of the Autun medallion and the loaf of bread or the cake is practically identical.

6. *Aquarius:* The vessel from which the water is flowing is curiously elongated.

7. *February:* A man warming himself in front of a fire.

8. *Pisces.*

9. *March:* Pruning. This and the previous four subjects are very similar to those at Vézelay, though there, in the medallion for February there are two figures.

10. *Aries.*

11. *April:* Animals being fed with branches. This is an unusual subject, but is, however, found at Vézelay also, in almost the same form.

12. *Taurus.*

13. *May:* Knight with a horse.

14. *Gemini.*

15. *Annus:* Until this point each occupation is followed by its corresponding month. To the right of this medallion, the order is reversed and the signs of the zodiac precede the occupations.

16. *Cancer.*

17. *June:* Eating fruit.

18. *Leo.*

19. *July:* Reaping. A man sharpens his scythe.

20. *Virgo.*

21. *August:* Threshing. A very similar subject exists at Vézelay.

22. *Libra.*

23. *September:* Vine harvest. A seated man gathers grapes, while he crushes the harvest with his bare feet in a wine-vat.

24. *Scorpio.*

25. *October:* Feeding hogs. A man strikes the branches of an oak tree with a stick to bring down the acorns.

26. *Sagittarius.*

27. *November:* Carrying fire-wood.

28. *Capricornus.*

29. *December:* Killing hogs for Christmas.

Between each pair of medallions, and partly hidden by their circular frames, are branches of foliage and flowers of various design. They also provide an interesting indication that the carving was done before the stones were set up in position. In many cases, the joins between the stones of the arch come near the point where the medallions join. If the carving had been done *in situ*, it would have been quite easy to disregard the joins in the stones and carry the carving across them. There are, however, several instances of a deliberate effort to avoid this. The sculptor obviously carved each stone separately, and tried to avoid carving the foliage on two adjoining stones, to save himself the difficult task of making the design fit perfectly.

[1] Webster, *op. cit.*, p. 169, pl. LV; *Reallexikon zur deutschen Kunstgeschichte*, vol. I, 1937, p. 715.

[2] Abbé Terret mentioned this possibility but without very much conviction (*Autun*, I, p. 107), but J. Adhémar (*Influences antiques dans l'art du Moyen Age français*, London, 1939, p. 196) identified the medallions correctly.

[3] Terret, *Autun*, I, p. 110.

MEASUREMENTS

Doorway: 5.52 m. wide
Lintel: 6.40 m. wide, 76.5 cm. high, 40 cm. thick
Tympanum: 6.40 m. wide, average thickness 35 cm.
Christ: 3.05 m. high
Signature of Gislebertus: 74 cm. wide, 5.5 cm. high

The proportions of the arches and columns have been modified in order to make the diagram of the tympanum clearer.

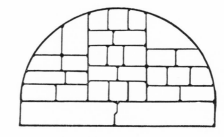

PLAN II.
STRUCTURE OF THE TYMPANUM

Diagram showing
the arrangement of stones in
the tympanum and lintel

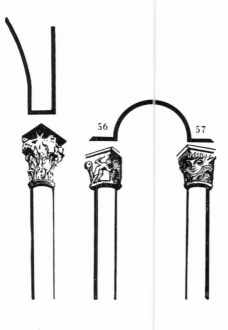

PLAN III. CAPITALS OF THE SIDE DOORWAYS

The tympanum of the west doorway

The letters and numbers used in plans I and III correspond with those of plates A-R (tympanum and lintel), O1-O31 (zodiac), S1-S6 (fragments of the inner arch), between pp. 32 and 57; and of plates 48-57 (capitals of the west doorways), between pp. 134 and 138.

A   Children clinging to an angel
(detail of the *lintel*)

B   The *tympanum:*
THE LAST JUDGEMENT
(showing the *lintel, arches* and *capitals*)

C   Souls entering paradise

D   St. Peter and the apostles

E   St. Peter at the gates of heaven

F, G   Angels supporting the mandorla; details of the garments of Christ

H, I   Christ in majesty

J   The weighing of souls: St. Michael and a devil

K   The gates of hell

L   Devils and damned

M   Paradise: the Virgin Mary enthroned

N   Paradise: two figures (Enoch and Elijah?)

O   *Zodiac*

1	Flower	4	Winter and Summer
2	Flower	5	January
3	Spring and Autumn	6	Aquarius

O	7	February	20	Virgo
	8	Pisces	21	August
	9	March	22	Libra
	10	Aries	23	September
	11	April	24	Scorpio
	12	Taurus	25	October
	13	May	26	Sagittarius
	14	Gemini	27	November
	15	Annus	28	Capricornus
	16	Cancer	29	December
	17	June	30	Flower
	18	Leo	31	Flower
	19	July		

P   The stranglehold of hell
(detail of the *lintel*)

Q   The *lintel:* the elect   (photo-montage)

R   The *lintel:* the damned   (photo-montage)

S   *Fragments of the inner arch*

1	Head of an elder of the Apocalypse	4	Musical instrument
2	Head of an angel (possibly from the north doorway)	5	Head (possibly from the north doorway)
3	Chalice	6	Head of an elder of the Apocalypse

Capitals of the west doorways

Plates 48-57 follow those illustrating the capitals of the interior (between pp. 134 and 138). The originals of 48 and 49 are in the 'Salle Capitulaire'; that of 50, in the Musée Rolin.

48   ETHIOPIAN (?)

49   BALAAM

50   TWO ATLANTES

51a   THE WOLF AND THE CRANE

51b   ABRAHAM DISMISSING HAGAR AND ISHMAEL

51c   SIX ELDERS OF THE APOCALYPSE

52a   THE PURIFICATION OF THE VIRGIN and THE PRESENTATION IN THE TEMPLE

52b   THE CONVERSION OF ST. EUSTACE

52c   ST. JEROME AND THE LION

53   DAVID AND HIS SLING

54   DAVID AND GOLIATH

55   WARRIOR

[Foliage capital, not reproduced among the plates]

56   YOUNG MAN AND MONKEY

57   HEAD OF A MONSTER

The second or middle arch of the central doorway is decorated with foliage which consists of two prominent wavy branches with leaves and flowers. The branches spring out from each end of the arch and meet at the apex. The arch itself is roll-moulded and the branches are carved in prominent relief. Along much of their length they are completely detached from the background. The branches are enriched with beading and they form half-circles as they meander along the arch. Each half-circle contains a few leaves and flowers, usually three, branching off the main stalks. The flowers and leaves are of a very similar general design throughout, though there is much variety in the details. The size of the semicircles on the left half of the arch is slightly smaller than on the right; thus the branch makes fourteen semi-circles on the left half while only twelve on the right. It is unlikely that any detailed design of the decoration of this arch existed beforehand. The sculptor carved the foliage with great freedom and with remarkable skill.

The two lateral doorways on the façade of Vézelay have outer arches carved with somewhat similar foliage motives and the arch of the south doorway, in particular, has a close parallel in Autun. At Vézelay, too, there are two branches which meet at the apex of the arch where, however, they are bound together and do not cross each other as at Autun. But it is the doorway at Anzy-le-Duc that provides the most striking comparison with Autun. There, not only the form of the foliage but the style of carving is very similar to Autun.[1]

As we shall see shortly, the original decoration of the inner arch at Autun probably resembled that of the corresponding one at Anzy-le-Duc. Now devoid of sculptural decoration, this blank inner arch enclosing the Autun tympanum is optically disturbing and we sense at once that it could not have been the original arrangement.

Abbé Devoucoux, in his book published in 1845,[2] refers to the arch in this way: 'The twelve patriarchs and the twelve prophets were represented on its curve; fragments of these figures broken off during the unfortunate restorations of 1760 [i.e. 1766, see note 4 on p. 25], have been found but are too damaged to be restored to their original position.' On reading this, an important question at once comes to mind. If the arch was destroyed in 1766 and only fragments of it existed in 1845, how did Abbé Devoucoux know that the arch was decorated with twelve figures of patriarchs and twelve of prophets? Did he know a drawing of the doorway made before 1766? If so, he would surely have mentioned it. He could not have relied on a local tradition or memory, for nobody at Autun seems to have been aware of the existence of the doorway hidden under the plaster until Abbé Devoucoux himself discovered it. It seems, therefore, that, on examining the fragments, he came to the conclusion

that the subjects they represented were the patriarchs and the prophets. Some of these fragments are probably among the heads and other subjects recently found in an upper storeroom of the cathedral. Amongst the heads, there are nine with crowns, two with caps and five without any headgear. There is, of course, no certainty that they all belonged to the destroyed arch of the central doorway. On the contrary, it is very likely that some formed part of the decoration of the north doorway, for we know that one of the arches there was decorated with carvings of angels. Amongst the fragments still surviving, there are six citharas or citterns of different forms, some with portions of the figures who held them. There are also four chalices with the hands which support them. These citharas and chalices make it quite obvious that they belonged to the elders of the Apocalypse and that the crowned heads are those of the elders. The blank arch of the central doorway rests, on the north side, on a capital which has as its decoration figures of six elders of the Apocalypse. It seems legitimate to assume that these figures completed the number of elders carved on the arch. If so, there must have been eighteen elders on the arch, to make up the traditional number of twenty-four.

We reproduce a selection of important elements from this series of fragments [pls. S1-6]. Two are heads with diadems, one of them bearded; these are obviously the elders of the Apocalypse from the west doorway. The upper part of the figure with a cithara, and a fragment showing the chalice supported by a hand, also, no doubt, came from the inner arch of the central doorway, since the chalice and a musical instrument were the usual attributes of the elders. One of the other two heads reproduced wears a cap and may come from the original tympanum over the door of the north transept. The other is probably the head of an angel from the inner arch of the same doorway. (One of these angels [pl. VII] is now in the Metropolitan Museum, New York, but its head is too damaged for the features to be made out.) We are fortunate in being able to gain some idea from these fragments of the original appearance of the inner arches over both doorways. (See plans I and IX.)

Two important doorways with the elders of the Apocalypse carved on them can be quoted as certainly preceding Autun. One is the great west door (1109-15), now destroyed, of Cluny Abbey on which the heads of the elders were carved within the twenty-four medallions of the outer arch.[3] Even more important as a possible model for Autun is the doorway at Anzy-le-Duc,[4] on which the whole figures of the elders with their musical instruments are carved on the inner arch. The carving is very damaged and difficult to decipher but it seems that not all the figures were fitted into the arch and some were, as at Autun, carved on one of the capitals below.

[1] This arch is now restored but photographs exist showing it before its restoration. See, for instance, V. Terret, *La sculpture bourguignonne aux XIIe et XIIIe siècles, Cluny,* Autun-Paris, 1914, pl. XXIX. (This work will be referred to from now on as: Terret, *Cluny.*)

[2] Devoucoux, *op. cit.*, p. 37.

[3] K. J. Conant, *The Third Church at Cluny,* in *Medieval Studies in Memory of A. Kingsley Porter,* Cambridge (U.S.A.), 1959, p. 335.

[4] Terret, *Cluny,* pl. XXIX; M. Aubert, *La Bourgogne,* Paris, 1930, vol. III, pp. 202-03.

PLS. A-S: *The tympanum, lintel and arches of the west doorway*

ICANI EI SINE FIN

D

37

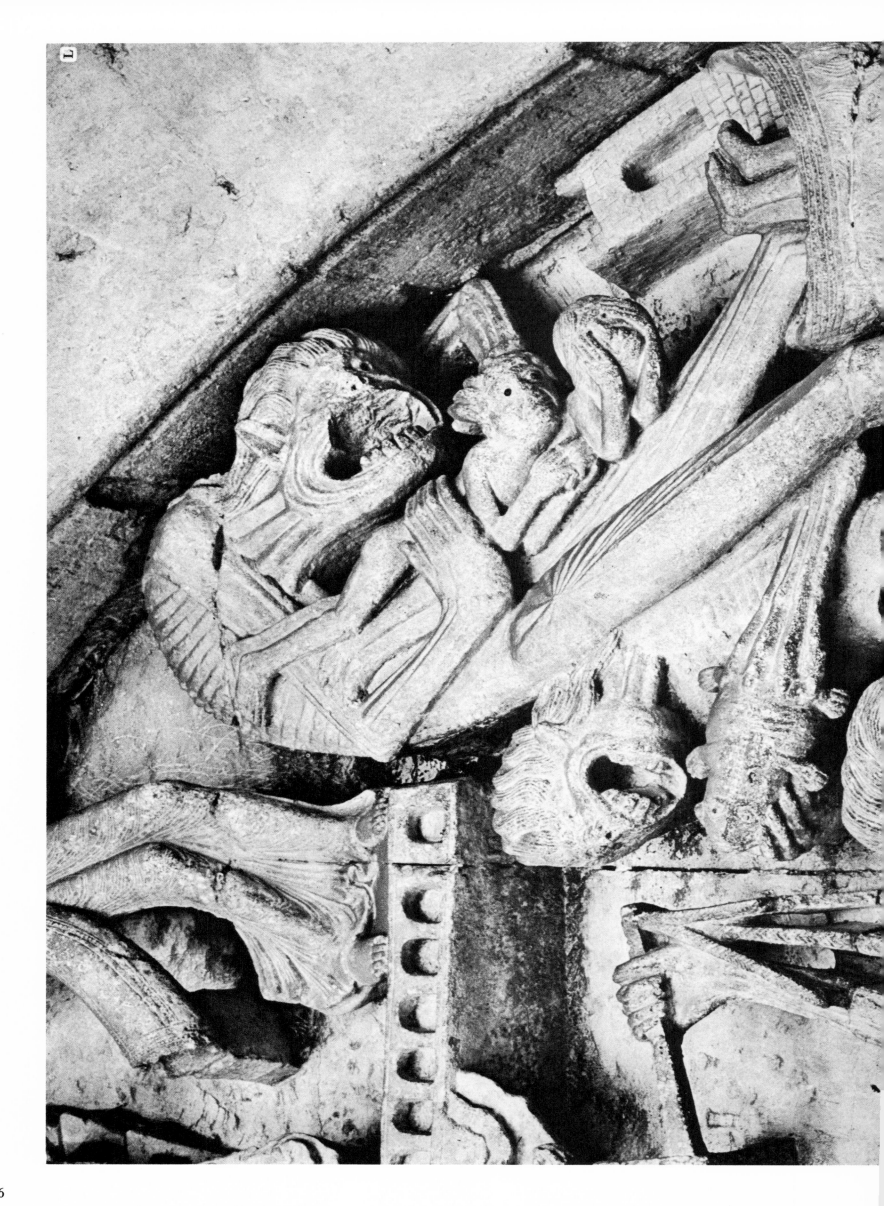

M

N

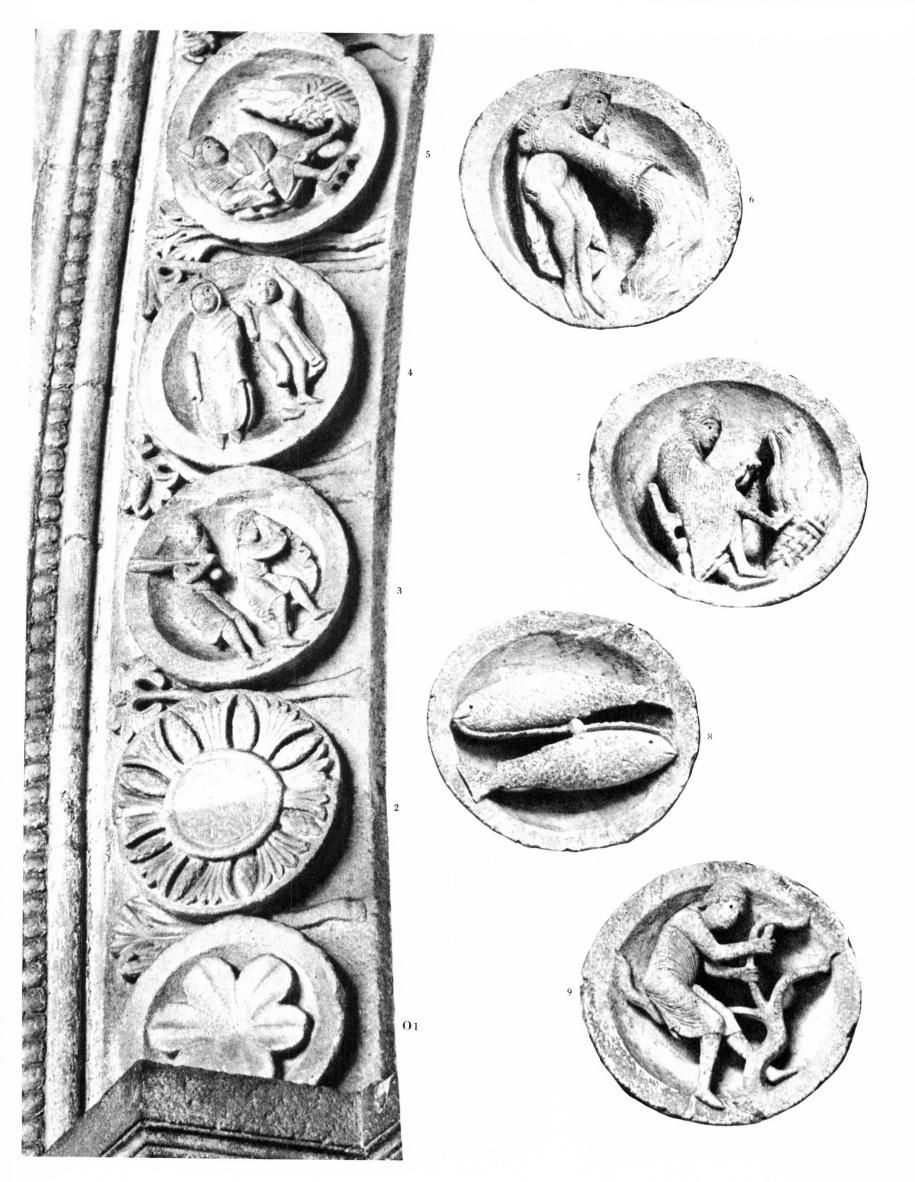

5

4

3

2

O 1

6

7

8

9

49

13

14

15

O 10

11

20

16

17

18

12

19

21

22

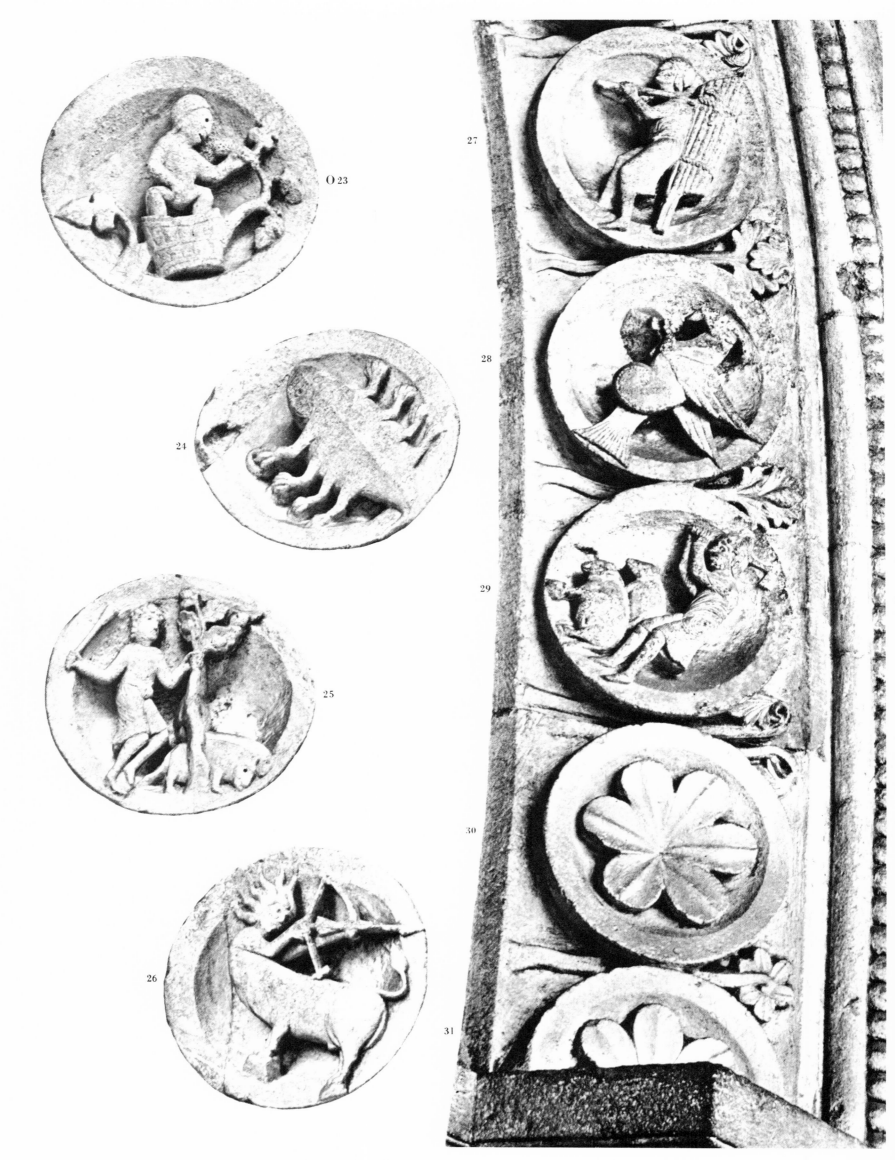

O 23

24

25

26

27

28

29

30

31

52

R

S 1

2

3

4

5

6

The capitals of the apse, choir, nave and west doorways

IN 1939, as we have already mentioned,[1] the marble cover of the apse was removed, revealing a well-preserved original work of the 12th century [pl. Ⓐ]. This original structure extends from the ground to the uppermost windows which, like the vaulting of the apse, are Gothic intrusions.

The 12th-century apse is divided horizontally by moulded and billet string-courses into three parts of which the lowest is a solid, plain plinth [plan IV, p. 142]. The two storeys above have five windows each and a blind arcade at either end. There are considerable and important differences between these two storeys, suggesting that there was a change of plans while the apse was being built. The blind arcades and the windows are flanked by fluted pilasters, which are carried up the whole height of the original structure and are crowned by capitals. The design of these pilasters changes at the top of the first storey. Below, they have four flutes, each flute being filled in with a roll-moulding, while above there are only three flutes and they are concave. The pilasters of the side apses are of the first type, with four flutes, and thus it can be assumed that they were built at the same time as the lower part of the main apse.

The change in the building plan is seen most clearly when examining the way in which the apse wall joins the choir. Both the string-courses which divide the storeys end abruptly and are not continued in the choir, as no doubt was first intended. The string-course above the second storey, on the other hand, is met by the capital of the first pilaster of the choir and it is obvious that, at this level, the apse and the choir were planned as one whole by the same architect.

The change of plans and craftsmen during the building of the apse also brought about a change in the style of the sculptural decoration. The first scheme provided the decoration of the engaged capitals of the blind arcades and of the windows—fourteen capitals in all[2]—and the carved labels over the windows. These last do not fit well and had to be cut off to make room for the pilasters. It is difficult to reconcile the technical competence of the carving of these labels with such a striking inability or carelessness in fitting them in place. The carving was done before the stones were put into position as there are some obvious misfits in the design. The decoration of these arches consists of the billet and the beaded patterns combined with palmettes and other floral motifs repeated uniformly along the whole curve. The carving is delicate and no doubt inspired by classical sources.

The capitals deserve special attention for they were carved in a style that combines two distinct traditions. One of these was widely used at the end of the 11th century and at the beginning of the 12th century in Burgundy, particularly in the Brionnais region.[3] It combines very simple upright acanthus leaves, long, graceless and stiff, with figure sculpture of a very simple form, chiefly confronted or addossed lions. The second style is derived from Cluny Abbey and consists of crisp acanthus leaves deeply undercut, with the characteristic hollowing out of the centre of the leaves. The style was used at Cluny in carving the celebrated capitals of the ambulatory and the numerous capitals of the south transept, and thus dates from shortly before 1100.[4]

The capitals of the 'Brionnais' style, apart from those at Autun, are always of a square shape at the top, while all the important capitals at Cluny are much more classical in form, having a cylindrical core and concave impost with rosettes in the centre. It is interesting to see that in the apse of St. Lazarus, even the 'Brionnais' style is applied, with one or two exceptions, to capitals of antique form. Here in fact the two styles mingle together quite happily. It seems that the carver or carvers of these capitals, though brought up in the 'Brionnais' tradition, were trying to bring the style of their sculpture up to date by the inclusion of elements they had learnt at Cluny. The peculiar form of the pilasters found in the plinth and first storey, however, is not found at Cluny but was, of course, a common Roman form used at the lower length of every fluted pilaster (see pls. Ⓐ, Ⓐ7). This suggests that the Autun sculptors made a study of Roman models independently of Cluny and it is possible that even the acanthus form they used, so close to that associated with Cluny, was derived directly from Roman sources. There are still a number of antique capitals at Autun, showing the crisp acanthus with 'hollows', exactly as on the apse capitals.

Among the capitals of the first storey, there is one which is decorated not only with the acanthus but also

---

[1] See pp. 14 and 19.

[2] Two of these capitals, those of the central window, are missing. A capital carved on two sides only with four lions and preserved in the Musée Rolin may well be one of them.

[3] Terret (*Autun*, I, p. 28) quotes as the examples of this style the capitals at Anzy-le-Duc and two capitals in the Musée Lapidaire at Autun (his pl. XI). G. Von Lucken (*Die Anfänge der burgundischen Schule, Ein Beitrag zum Aufleben des Antike in der Baukunst des XII. Jahrhunderts*, Basle (no date) illustrates as examples of this style capitals from Anzy-le-Duc, Vézelay, Tournus, Charlieu, Bois-Ste.-Marie, Issy-l'Évêque, Mont-St.-Vincent, Gourdon, La Charité. See also: P. Deschamps (*Notes sur la sculpture romane en Bourgogne*, in *Gazette des Beaux-Arts*, 1922, vol. 22, p. 73) and F. Salet (*op. cit.*, p. 146).

[4] We accept the early dating of the Cluny ambulatory capitals, i.e., before 1095. For the transept we accept the date between 1095 and 1100. Many of the small and insignificant capitals of the south transept (K. J. Conant, *Medieval Academy Excavations at Cluny, III*, in *Speculum*, IV, 1929, pp. 291-302, and plates) could not have been carved *in situ;* it would have been a technical impossibility. Their date must, therefore, be before 1100. Once this fact is accepted, all the other transept capitals must be of the same date, for they form a fairly homogeneous group.

with a nude figure (its head is broken off) piercing itself with a sword [pl. Ⓐ1]. It is undoubtedly *Ira* (Anger), one of the Vices from Prudentius' *Psychomachia*.[1] This isolated representation, taken out of its context, has no other than a decorative significance. As will be seen later, one of the capitals of the nave has an almost identical figure [pl. 19], but there it is used with the corresponding figure of a Virtue. We know that the small ambulatory capitals at Cluny were illustrations of the *Psychomachia* and it is more than likely that the Autun capital was inspired by one of these.

Another of the choir capitals is carved with an *Owl* [pl. Ⓐ4]. Here too, the model seems to have been provided by Cluny. This is suggested by the shape of the capital, as well as by a detail which is typical of Cluny. This is a rosette or flower which is placed in the centre of a concave impost. Such a rosette was the usual embellishment of a Corinthian capital, but at Cluny a vertical stem was added to the rosette, such as is found on the *Owl* capital at Autun.

The decoration of the second storey is confined to the large, flat capitals of the pilasters. Unfortunately, the relief of these capitals projected too much and was crudely cut off when the marble cover of the apse was erected in the 18th century. Of the eight capitals, two are completely ruined; of the three which were carved with foliage motives, only one is fairly well preserved. The remaining three were decorated with figure subjects; of these, one consisted of several figures, of which one was an angel [pl. Ⓐ6]. This series of capitals differs from the capitals of the first storey in its superior quality.

The most interesting and important is the third capital

from the north [pl. Ⓐ5] which, though badly mutilated, still shows enough to give a sufficient idea of the subject and style. In the centre is a figure seated on a throne, resting its feet on an arch made of three concentric, beaded bands. The sides of the capital had acanthus foliage of the Corinthian type, but this is very badly damaged. The enthroned figure, probably *Christ*, is carved with infinite delicacy. The modelling of the body, the intricate decorative folds, the characteristic structure of the limbs show at first glance that it is the work of the sculptor who carved the Christ of the west tympanum—Gislebertus. This fact has very important implications: *it can hardly be doubted that the apse capitals of the second storey were the first to be carved by Gislebertus on his arrival at Autun; yet the style of these first works does not substantially differ from the last of Gislebertus's sculptures, those of the west front.* The deductions which can be drawn from this observation will be discussed in the last chapter.

There can be no doubt that the first workshop set up for the building of the church of St. Lazarus, and responsible for the plinth and the first storey of the apse, owed something to the inspiration of Cluny. With the setting up of the second workshop and the arrival of Gislebertus, this contact became much stronger. Not only was the design of the pilasters altered to conform to the Cluny model, but also the blind niches were to receive an enrichment which was used at Cluny throughout the church, namely the cusped mouldings. The north blind arcade at Autun is unfinished, but the south has the cusped moulding precisely like that which is still preserved in the transept of Cluny [pls. Ⓐ8 and Ⓐ9].

The capitals of the choir and nave[2]

THE FOUR RIVERS OF PARADISE [pl. 1]. 'And a river went out of Eden to water the garden; and from thence it was parted and became into four heads.'

Medieval artists frequently illustrated this passage from *Genesis*[3] by depicting the four rivers as four figures holding vessels of various shapes from which they are pouring water. It is clear that this representation of the four rivers is derived from classical sources such as the representations of the river-gods and Aquarius, one of the signs of the zodiac.

[1] Aurelius Prudentius Clemens, born about 348 in northern Spain, wrote shortly before 410 the *Psychomachia* (the War of the Souls)—an allegorical poem describing the struggle between duty and passion, the Virtues and the Vices, ending with a victory for the Virtues. The *Psychomachia* became one of the most popular writings of the Middle Ages. (See: R. Stettiner, *Die Illustrierten Prudentiushandschriften*, Berlin, 1895 and 1905; also H. Woodruff, *The Illustrated Manuscript of Prudentius*, in *Art Studies*, 1929, pp. 33-79.)

[2] As a general rule, the plates are arranged to follow the order in which the capitals were erected, from east to west. The textual descriptions do not always follow this plan and have sometimes been grouped according to subject matter and iconography.

[3] II, 10-14. For a general discussion of this theme, see E. Schlee, *Die Ikonographie der Paradiesesflüsse*, Leipzig, 1937.

Gislebertus displayed great originality in his composition: having a comparatively flat capital of a pilaster at his disposal, with only one large surface available for carving, he placed two of his figural representations of the rivers at angles (the left-hand side figure is a modern restoration in stucco), and these support the abacus with their heads, like caryatids. The other two figures are much smaller and hold their vessels above their heads. All four figures have diadems on their heads and are nude save for a cloak thrown over their shoulders. The *Aquarius* over the west tympanum [pl. O6] is carved in an exactly similar manner except that there the diadem is replaced by a cap. The figures of the rivers are singularly graceful, especially the one which stands crosslegged, in a pose suggesting delightful happiness.

Besides the Autun capital, there are three others in Burgundy carved with this subject. The famous capital at Cluny is probably the oldest, and no doubt started the fashion. In common with the *Four Rivers* of Autun, it has an abacus of which one member is concave, while the core of the capital, behind the carving, is convex.

The Magi before Herod
(detail pl. 10)
Pls. Ⓐ-Ⓐ10: *The main apse and its capitals*

Ⓐ1

Ⓐ2

Ⓐ3

Ⓐ4

Ⓐ5

Ⓐ

60

Ⓐ6

Ⓐ7

Ⓐ View of the apse today

Ⓐ1-Ⓐ4 Lower-level capitals, not by Gislebertus

Ⓐ5, Ⓐ6 Upper-level capitals, by Gislebertus

Ⓐ7 Porte d'Arroux, Autun (Roman)
cf. the use of fluted pilasters in St. Lazarus, pl. Ⓐ and pl. facing p. 141

Ⓐ8 Cusped moulding, Autun

Ⓐ9 Cusped moulding, Cluny

Ⓐ10 The apse before removal of the 18th-century marble covering in 1939

Ⓐ10

Ⓐ9

Ⓐ8

Ⓑ1 Moûtiers-St.-Jean: *The Journey to Emmaus*

Ⓑ2 Autun (Gislebertus): *The Journey to Emmaus*

Ⓑ4 Autun (Master of Moûtiers-St.-Jean): *Christ Washing the Apostles' Feet*

Ⓑ3 *The Journey to Emmaus*—Christ as a pilgrim *(St. Albans Psalter)*

Ⓑ5 Moûtiers-St.-Jean: *Samson and the Lion*

Ⓑ6 Autun (Master of Moûtiers-St.-Jean): *Samson and the Lion*

In all other respects, the treatment of the Cluny capital is different and, in fact, all four Burgundian examples are so unlike each other that it is difficult to imagine any but the most distant relationship between them.

The other two capitals depicting the *Rivers of Paradise* in Burgundy are at Anzy-le-Duc and Vézelay. The first has two figures only, seated and holding horn-like vessels. At Vézelay, the figures crouch or sit. In common with Cluny, the figures on these capitals are placed between trees, a motif which is entirely lacking at Autun.

But if the Autun capital does not follow closely the composition of the Cluny capital, its placing in the extreme east part of the church repeats the position of the Cluny capital, which was prominently situated in the ambulatory.

THE JOURNEY TO EMMAUS [pl. 2]. The story carved on this capital has hitherto always been thought to represent the 'Healing of the Blind Man of Jericho'.[1] The capital has been extensively restored and it seems that the restorers, believing this interpretation to be correct, added a few details which increased the confusion. (See fig. 2, p. 82.)

The identification of the scene was made on the grounds that the little figure to the right, opening the door and standing on a tree, is Zacchaeus, the publican of Jericho, who climbed up a sycamore tree to see Jesus in a crowd. This episode and that of the healing of the blind man are described in the Gospel of St. Luke.[2]

There are several objections to this identification. All the Autun capitals illustrate one and one scene only, or at most, as in the case of *Jacob* [pl. 26] or *St. Peter in Chains* [pl. 33], two or three incidents of the same story. The healing of the blind man and the story of Zacchaeus are two distinct narratives, although they follow each other in St. Luke's Gospel. The second objection is that the 'blind man' has a nimbus which is original and not a restoration. This clearly is quite unjustifiable, and should warn us against accepting the orthodox identification of the scene.

A further objection is that Christ is here represented as a pilgrim. This is unmistakable as he has a pilgrim's scrip and a pilgrim's staff. The staff is of a characteristic form, as if two sticks were bound together with leather straps or ribbons. The two pilgrims on the lintel of the west doorway each carry exactly this kind of staff and scrip [pl. Q]. On a capital in the south nave arcade, a pilgrim is represented with the same attributes [pl. 16]. It is perfectly obvious that there is no reason to represent Christ as a pilgrim if the scene is the 'Healing of the Blind Man of Jericho'. There is, however, a scene in which he is frequently so depicted. It is the *Journey to Emmaus* as described by St. Luke.[3] The reliefs showing this subject in the cloisters at Arles in Provence and at Silos in Spain show Christ with staff and scrip. In manuscript painting and in stained glass too, this iconography seems

to have been accepted. For instance, one of the illuminations in the *St. Albans Psalter* (fol. 69 vº) illustrating the *Journey to Emmaus* shows Christ with a scrip and staff of exactly the same form as on the Autun capital [pl. ⒷB3], and a similar scene occurs amongst the windows of Chartres.[4]

However, the surest proof that Gislebertus carved this scene and not the 'Healing of the Blind Man' is the capital from Moûtiers-Saint-Jean (Côte-d'Or) now in the Fogg Museum, Cambridge (U.S.A.) [pl. ⒷB1]. This, as all other capitals from that church, is closely connected with Gislebertus's style, and it represents the *Journey to Emmaus*. Here, not only is Christ shown as a pilgrim with a staff of the right form (though without a scrip) but the two disciples have travellers' stocks. The head of one of the disciples is broken off but it is clear that he was making a gesture similar to that of the 'blind man' on the Autun capital. The composition and the gestures of the figures in both cases, if we make allowances for the restorations of the Autun capital, are almost identical. To the right of the scene on the Moûtiers-Saint-Jean capital, is a house from which a half-figure with a drinking horn is leaning. At Autun, this detail is only slightly different: the figure leaning out of a building has no horn, and there is another little figure opening the door. This is the illustration of Emmaus where the two disciples were to spend the night. 'And they drew nigh unto the village, whither they went; and he made as though he would have gone further. But they constrained him saying. Abide with us: for it is toward evening, and the day is far spent. And he went in to tarry with them.'[5] The little figure opening the door is obviously intended to represent an inn-keeper, and the foliage on which he stands is nothing but a conventional support,[6] just as the figure of the angel to the left of Christ has a long branch of acanthus under its feet. (Incidentally, an almost identical figure of an angel is found in exactly the same position on the Moûtiers-Saint-Jean capital, which makes the similarity between the two works even closer.) Most figures in Gislebertus's work have some artificial form of support. Usually this takes the shape of a little cushion-like projection; sometimes it is a kind of arcaded stool; occasionally, it is a branch of foliage (*Death of Cain* [pl. 18], *St. Vincent* [pl. 41]).

The particular significance of the connection between Autun and Moûtiers-Saint-Jean lies in the fact that the two capitals in the south arcade of the Autun nave, (the *Washing of the Feet* [pl. 31] and *Samson and the Lion* [pl. 29]), which are clearly not by Gislebertus, are so close in style to the Moûtiers-Saint-Jean capitals that it is probable the same master carved them. *It is likely, therefore, that he was one of the assistants of Gislebertus and thus acquired an intimate knowledge of the Autun capitals.*[7]

---

[1] Terret, *Autun*, II, p. 42.
[2] XVIII, 35-42.
[3] XXIV, 13-35.

[4] Pächt, Dodwell and Wormald, *The St. Albans Psalter*, London, 1960, [pl. 38; Mâle, *op. cit.*, fig. 117.
[5] *Luke*, XXIV, 28-29.
[6] At Vézelay there are a few instances of the use of arcaded supports for figures, but in most cases figures stand on branches of foliage or on the plain, slanting ground.
[7] See pp. 73 and 176.

PLS. Ⓑ1-Ⓑ6: *Comparative plates, Autun and Moûtiers-Saint-Jean*

In spite of its unfortunate restoration, the *Journey to Emmaus* is one of the most delightful capitals at Autun. The agitation of the figures is matched perfectly by the draperies, full of unexpected twists and carved with brilliant delicacy. The peculiar treatment of the thighs of the two apostles should be noted. The cloth adheres here closely to the body and a peculiar enrichment is introduced, namely horizontal, beaded bands and a small, incised cross. This peculiarity appears on the figure of the angel in the *Annunciation* scene [pl. 47] and also on the figures of the Archangel Michael [pl. J] and the angels supporting the mandorla on the tympanum of the west doorway [pls. F and G].

The eyes in these heads which are original and not restored are drilled and filled with dark blue paste. Unfortunately, this technique was not very successful and the paste often fell out, as can be seen in numerous cases at Autun and elsewhere.

In our final remarks on the iconography we shall return to the subject of this capital to discuss its connection with medieval mystery plays.

THE FIRST TEMPTATION OF CHRIST [pl. 3]. There are two capitals at Autun illustrating the temptations of Christ.[1] The choir capital shows the episode described by St. Matthew in which Christ, after having fasted for forty days and nights, feels hungry and is being tempted by the devil to change stone into bread.[2]

Unfortunately, this capital is extensively restored (see fig. 3, p. 82): most of the figure of Christ and of the angel behind him is of stucco. So is the plant below the platform on which Christ stands. The devil's hands and claws are also modern. In repairing this capital, the restorers no doubt used as a model one of the capitals at Saulieu, which is, like all the others there, a free copy of a prototype at Autun. At Saulieu, the devil also holds a stone in his hands, from which we can be reasonably certain that this detail at Autun is quite trustworthy. (See pl. ⒹÐ7 and p. 175.)

Since the temptation took place in the wilderness, the sculptor carved numerous branches to give an impression of bushes. The only figure preserved largely intact is that of the devil. He is a winged creature with flame-like hair, a monstrous mouth and a body covered with wisps of hair. His symbol, the snake, coils round his legs. The medieval mind was preoccupied with visions of hell, devils and monsters of every kind and shape. No wonder, therefore, that the artists of the period showed such an inventiveness in depicting devils.

LUXURIA [pl. 4]. The capital facing the *Journey to Emmaus*, on the west side of the same arcade, was identified by Abbé Terret as the 'Massacre of the Innocents',[3] while Émile Mâle suggested, much more convincingly, that the subject was that of a young man contemplating

a nude woman and thus becoming the victim of a demon.[4] The capital is unique in its subject, but it seems obvious that the interpretation of that great scholar, Émile Mâle, is correct, and that the intention of the sculptor was to stigmatise the vice of sensuality. The subject can well be called, therefore, as he proposed, *Luxuria* (Lechery).

The capital was restored in the 19th century but it seems that the restoration affects only the surface of certain parts of the carving. This can be deduced from the description of the capital by Abbé Devoucoux made before 1845 and thus before the restoration, in which he mentions all the details as they appear today, including the axe or hammer of the demon.[5]

If the meaning of the composition as a whole is fairly easily understood, the details seem at first sight incomprehensible. Why, for instance, is the nude woman's hair carved in the shape of a fantastic wreath, and why is she holding a round object in one hand and a curved knife or scroll in another? The demon brandishes an axe or hammer—the only case of a devil holding such a tool, at least at Autun.

It is our belief that the explanation of all these peculiarities is found in medieval representations of the pagan gods. One of the late copies of the 12th-century treatise called the *Liber ymaginum deorum*[6] is illustrated with pen drawings made in about 1420. One of these [pl. ⒷB19] represents Venus with a wreath on her head, a shell in one hand and a bow in another. To her right is Vulcan with a hammer and to her left, Cupid. The scene has still further participants, including the three Graces. Of course Gislebertus could not have anticipated this illustration, nor was he likely to have known the *Liber ymaginum deorum*, especially as it was probably written at the end of the 12th century.[7] However, he was likely to have seen a representation of Venus and Vulcan in which the pagan gods were given evil characteristics. The nude Venus became the temptress, but her attributes were misunderstood; the shell was taken for a stone and the bow which she held with Cupid was taken to represent a knife. Cupid himself was transformed into an innocent youth, and Vulcan, while retaining his hammer, was given the form of a devil.

Such transformations of the pagan gods and the heroes of ancient mythology were frequent in the Middle Ages. They are usually degraded to the roles of devils' accomplices or even devils themselves.[8]

It is not surprising to find a capital with this kind of allegorical representation at Autun, and also to find it in this particular place, within the choir. At Cluny, the capitals on the wall around the ambulatory were carved with the representations of the Virtues and Vices and

---

[1] For the *Second Temptation*, see p. 73, pl. 28.
[2] IV, 1-4.
[3] Terret, *Autun*, II, p. 40.

[4] Mâle, *op. cit.*, p. 374.
[5] *op. cit.*, p. 59.
[6] Vatican Library, *Cod. Reginensis*, 1290.
[7] For a discussion of the authorship of this MS. see: J. Seznec, *La Survivance des dieux antiques*, in *Studies of the Warburg Institute*, vol. XI, London, 1940, pp. 147 *seq.*
[8] R. Hamann, *Diana and the Snake-Tongued Demon*, in the *Burlington Magazine*, vol. LXI, 1932, p. 207.

since Autun shows numerous signs of having been influenced by Cluny, it is not improbable that Gislebertus based his capitals on a model which existed there. The figures of the Autun capital are placed against a background of Corinthian foliage with a leaf on a long stalk in the centre, where, on the true Corinthian capital, there would have been a rosette. Such leaves or flowers on long stalks are characteristic of most Cluny capitals.

CONSTANTINE (?) [pl. 6]. Opposite the *First Temptation of Christ* [pl. 3], on the west side of the same arch, is a capital showing a rider trampling on a nude figure. The horseman is a king or an emperor wearing a diadem and dressed in a rich tunic with a coat over it.

It has been suggested that this is one of the 12th-century imitations of the equestrian statue of Marcus Aurelius on the Capitol in Rome, which was, during the Middle Ages, placed in front of the basilica of St. John the Lateran and believed to be the monument of Constantine the Great.[1] At that time the horse was supposed to be trampling on a barbarian, who was interpreted as a symbol of defeated paganism. There are very strong arguments supporting the idea that some of the 12th-century equestrian figures, especially in western France, were representations of Constantine. But, as Professor Crozet has wisely remarked 'two or even several apparently similar representations may stem from different sources and have a different significance'.[2]

The Autun horseman is an isolated example in Burgundy and it is impossible to be at all certain whether he really was modelled on the example of the Roman statue, though perhaps the fact that Constantine visited Autun (Augustodunum) in 311 supports such an interpretation. Whatever the ultimate source of this representation, however, it is likely that the capital was designed to conform to the whole allegorical programme of the decoration of this part of the church. Whether its meaning was the triumph of the Christian faith over paganism or whether it was designed to stigmatise Pride, as suggested by Abbé Terret,[3] or was yet some other subject altogether, it is impossible to guess.

The horseman on the capital is shown against a background of luxuriant foliage and flowers or fruit. In this case, the horse and the crouching nude figure have no supports under their feet unlike most other Autun capitals. There is something very naïve in the doll-like figure of the horseman and the grotesque anatomy of the horse, and, at the same time, an extraordinary feeling for decorative quality in placing the head of the king at the exact spot where the central rosette should be, while the flowers replace the usual volutes of the Corinthian capital.

The progress of the building makes it obvious that the capitals of the choir must have been carved quickly one

after the other. This is certainly confirmed by their stylistic similarities. They seem also to be connected with each other, or at least most of them, by their allegorical subjects, in which temptation and resistance to temptation play a prominent part. The *First Temptation of Christ* [pl. 3] is the supreme example of the rejection of temptation. *Luxuria* [pl. 4] provides a contrast to the previous subject and a warning to the faithful not to succumb. A group of capitals in close proximity to the *First Temptation of Christ*, all on the south side of the church, seem to relate, in their subjects, to this central idea of the contrast between good and evil. The interpretation of these subjects is not easy and there remains much uncertainty as to their exact meaning.

The four capitals which will now be described form a closely connected group. Only one of them [pl. 24] is still in its original position on the south side of the south apse arch. The other three [pls. 7, 8, 9] are in the 'Salle Capitulaire'; they were removed during the restoration, probably in 1858,[4] and replaced by copies. (See plans V and VI, pp. 142 and 143.)

MAN RIDING A BIRD [pl. 7]. This capital was placed on the same pier as *Constantine* but it was facing south.

A man sits astride a large cock-like bird, several times larger than himself, holding it with one hand, while in the other he has a sword ready for an attack. The figure is nude, except for a cap on his head.

The evil character of the bird is shown by its gigantic size in relation to the man. The scene is close in character to the other capitals of this group and has, no doubt, some allegorical meaning.[5]

THREE-HEADED BIRD [pl. 8]. Against a background of acanthus foliage, with angle volutes formed by fruit, a large bird is carved. The bird has three heads on long necks (one head has been broken off and a section of the right-hand neck is missing). The heads have curious collars or hoods, which project above the heads like ears. The legs are those of an aquatic bird.

This fantastic creature had great popularity among the sculptors of Burgundy, for it is found carved on the capitals of the main doorway at Vézelay [pl. Ⓑ15] and at Perrecy-les-Forges [pl. Ⓑ16].[6] At both those places, the three-headed bird is faced by other figures, a female faun

---

[1] The most recent study of this subject, with a full bibliography, is by R. Crozet, *Nouvelles remarques sur les cavaliers sculptés ou peints dans les églises romanes*, in *Cahiers de civilisation médiévale*, vol. I, 1958, p. 27.

[2] *op. cit.*, p. 36.

[3] Terret, *Autun*, II, pp. 21-22.

[4] This is the date mentioned in a document in the cathedral archives.

[5] The same motif of a nude man astride a bird was frequently employed by the sculptor Wiligelmo and his followers (R. Salvini, *Wiligelmo e le origini della scultura romanica*, Milan, 1954, see especially pl. 32). Burgundian influences in Romanesque sculpture in northern Italy were strong, so the motif may have come from Burgundy.

[6] F. Salet (*op. cit.*, p. 173) lists also an example at Montceaux-l'Étoile, but this seems to be an error. C. and A. M. Oursel (*Les Églises romanes de l'Autunois et du Brionnais*, Mâcon, 1956, p. 261, n. 1, mention Vézelay and Perrecy-les-Forges, but are not aware of the existence of the same subject at Autun. Three-headed birds are very seldom represented in art though three-headed monsters are found more frequently. M. Jurgis Baltrusaitis has kindly supplied the following references to works where pictures of three-headed animals occur: the *Rutland Psalter*, fol. 85, the *Luttrell Psalter*, fol. 190 v°, the *Bestiary* of Richard de Fournival in the Bibliothèque Ste.-Geneviève, MS. 2200, fol. 185 v°, and the *Moralium* of St. Gregory (12th cent.) in the Bibliothèque Communale at Amiens (MS. 38).

at Vézelay and a faun at Perrecy-les-Forges, both with a sling. In addition there is at Vézelay a siren with a woman's head, a bird's body and a serpent's tail.

The subject which is carved at Vézelay on one capital— the female faun, the three-headed bird and the siren— is found in a slightly modified form at Autun split between this and the following capital.

FAUN AND SIREN [pl. 24]. On the capital of the arch in front of the south apse, a faun with the feet of an aquatic bird, a sling in his right hand and a shield in his left, approaches a siren with a serpent's tail. The similarity with the capital at Vézelay [pl. Ⓑ15] is really striking but the clue to the understanding of both is found at Cluny. There, on the wall of the ambulatory, was a capital, now lost, but recorded in 1814 by van Riesamburgh [pl. Ⓑ12].[1] The capital showed a faun dressed only with a belt of fur holding a spherical shield and facing a three-headed bird. It can be assumed that the faun was holding a sling and that on the right face of the capital was a siren. In any case it is perfectly clear that Vézelay and Perrecy-les-Forges copied the Cluny model fairly faithfully and that Gislebertus, having only flat capitals at his disposal, divided the scene he knew from Cluny between this and the *Three-headed Bird* [pl. 8].

The meaning of the subject on the Cluny capital and of its derivatives is not clear, though it is thought to have been connected with the *Psychomachia*.[2] There can be little doubt, however, that its ultimate source is classical mythology. Like Venus, Cupid and Vulcan in *Luxuria* [pl. 4], the faun and the siren acquired a new, chiefly demoniac meaning—the siren becoming the symbol of feminine temptation. How close the *Faun and Siren* capital is to its Cluny model can be seen even in such a detail as the ornament below the abacus. A similar ornament appears, though very faintly, on the Riesamburgh drawing.[4]

FIGHT WITH A BASILISK [pl. 9]. The last capital of this group was on the south side of the arcade leading from the transept to the south aisle of the choir. The original in the 'Salle Capitulaire' is very much damaged.

The basilisk, that composite creature, half-cock, half-serpent, was derived from classical mythology and was regarded by the men of the Middle Ages as an incarnation of the devil. On this particular capital the basilisk is being attacked by a nude figure sitting on the monster's tail, armed with a helmet, shield and sword, and by a centaur who discharges his arrow into the monster's

mouth. To the right of the centaur, another small nude figure is striking a blow at the serpent with a club.

There is a striking similarity between the little nude figure fighting the basilisk, the faun [pl. 24] and the man riding a bird [pl. 7]. Thus, it can be assumed that they symbolise the forces of good engaged in fighting evil, in the respective forms of the basilisk, the siren and the giant bird.

In contrast with the previous capitals of this group, the *Fight with a Basilisk* is carved on a plain background, with hardly any foliage. The figures stand on prominent round supports, decorated with rows of beading.

The infancy of Christ

The remaining capitals in the choir, carved with historiated subjects, are all placed on the north side. They are related to each other in their subjects, illustrating three episodes from the story of the Magi and the Flight into Egypt, as described in the Gospel of St. Matthew.[5] The capitals were obviously intended to be viewed on entering the church through the north entrance, for the first scene was placed on that side of the pier of the crossing which faces the north door. This is the *Magi before Herod* [pl. 10]. Facing it, on the north wall, is the second episode, the *Adoration of the Magi* [pl. 12]. On the east side of the north-east crossing pier is the *Dream of the Magi* [pl. 11], and opposite, the *Flight into Egypt* [pl. 5]. All four capitals are now in the 'Salle Capitulaire'; two only were replaced by copies; for some obscure reason, the *Magi before Herod* and the *Dream of the Magi* were not copied. (See plans V and VI, pp. 142 and 143.)

THE MAGI BEFORE HEROD [pl. 10]. This capital is very mutilated, and in recent times the heads of one of the Magi and of Herod have been stolen.[6]

The three Wise Men of the East, having arrived at Jerusalem and dismounted, are seen approaching the king of the Jews seated on a throne. All the figures are dressed in richly ornamented tunics and cloaks. Herod and one of the Magi wear diadems set with jewels.

Having heard from the Wise Men about the birth of Christ, Herod 'sent them to Bethlehem, and said: Go and search diligently for the young child; and when you have found him, bring me word again, that I may come and worship him also'.[7]

THE ADORATION OF THE MAGI [pl. 12]. The Virgin and Child, with St. Joseph, somewhat perplexed, behind them, are shown seated under a rich, arcaded structure. The Wise Men, led by a star, approach the

---

[1] K. J. Conant, *Medieval Academy Excavations at Cluny*, in *Speculum*, vol. XXIX, 1954, pl. xva. R. and A. M. Oursel, *op. cit.*, pp. 232 and 262, were the first to connect the capital from Perrecy-les-Forges with the Riesamburgh drawings from Cluny.

[2] Conant, *op. cit.*, p. 40.

[3] Hamann, *Diana and the Snake-Tongued Demon*, in the *Burlington Magazine*, vol. LXI, 1932, p. 207; Adhémar, *op. cit.*, p. 185.

[4] Fabius (Fabien) van Riesamburgh was a pupil of Ingres, and his sketch-book is in the Académie de Mâcon. The relevant drawing is on fol. 28 v°. We owe this information to the kindness of Professor Conant.

[5] II, 1-14.

[6] These heads can be seen in two photographs, one published by Terret (*Autun*, II, pl. XLI) and reproduced here [pl. 10c], and the other taken by Abbé Grivot [pl. 10b]. Pl. 10a shows the present state of the capital; it should be noted that the Wise Man nearest to Herod has been broken off at some time and replaced too high.

[7] *Matthew*, II, 8.

Child. One is about to kneel while presenting his gift; the second, who, without a beard, is the youngest of the three, lifts his crown in respect; while the third, in an attitude of reverence, waits for his turn to offer his gift.

According to St. Matthew, the gifts brought by the Wise Men consisted of gold, frankincense and myrrh.[1] The first two Magi hold their gifts in round containers but that of the third is in a box. It has been suggested that this is a book which, according to a legend found in apocryphal writings, was sealed by the hand of God and given by him to Adam and Eve. This book contained a promise of their salvation when Jesus had been born in Bethlehem. The book passed from Adam and Eve to their descendants until it came into the possession of Melkon, the king of Persia and one of the Wise Men.[2] The difficulty in accepting this hypothesis is that the object held by the third Wise Man at Autun is so obviously not a book but a box.[3] Moreover, on the tympanum at Neuilly-en-Donjon (Allier) two of the Magi have gifts of the same shape.

The *Adoration of the Magi* capital, although it is damaged and the bottom part missing, is an exquisite composition, full of touching tenderness.

THE DREAM OF THE MAGI [pl. 11].

'And being warned of God in a dream that they should not return to Herod, they departed into their own country another way.'[4]

The composition of the scene is delightfully naïve: it is seen at the same time from above (the heads of the Magi, asleep in their jewelled crowns), and from the side (their legs and the figure of the angel). Pointing to the star which is to lead them back to their homes, the messenger of God touches the hand of one of the Magi, who opens his eyes while his companions are still peacefully asleep. The concentric folds of the bed-clothes form a bold rythmic pattern. Gislebertus devoted much attention to the details: for instance, the underside of the bed, which is not visible on photographs, is so carefully carved that it is possible to study its construction, which consists of leather or rope straps as on a hammock, attached to a wooden frame; unfortunately, the turned bedposts are damaged.

This capital is the only sculpture at Autun still showing some minute traces of the original colours: red, blue, green and gold (for an analysis, see Appendix 1, p. 178).

At first sight the lower part of this capital, which is carved with foliage on a separate piece of stone, seems to be too wide to have been part of one and the same capital. However, on this lower section, in exactly the spot where the body of the angel would have been continued downwards, are traces of the mutilated form of the lower part of the angel's body, which proves that the two pieces

always belonged together. There are other capitals at Autun which are made of two pieces of stone, though in every case they are extremely well fitted together (e.g., the *Journey to Emmaus*, the *First Temptation of Christ* and *Luxuria*, all in the choir [pls. 2, 3, 4]).

THE FLIGHT INTO EGYPT [pl. 5].[5]

This is undoubtedly the most popular capital with visitors to Autun and the one most frequently illustrated.

St. Joseph leads the donkey by a rope; he is armed against any misadventure with a sword carried on his shoulder.[6] His open mouth seems to suggest fatigue from the long journey on foot. The Virgin and Child form a delightful, lyrical group: the mother holds her baby firmly with one hand while supporting a globe in the other; Jesus places his right hand on the globe as if conscious of his mission but with the other he holds tight to his mother's arm, still a helpless child. In the background are branches of foliage and fruit, and along the lower edge of the capital circular supports with beading are arranged in a regular row.

Supports of various shapes are extensively used on the Autun capitals, though this is the only example of such a regular repetition of supports of one shape for purely decorative purposes.[7] Three round, wheel-like supports are found, for instance, on the *Basilisk* capital [pl. 9], but they are not as regular as in the *Flight into Egypt*. Nevertheless, there is no need to explain them as being influenced by other techniques, embroidery for instance, as is often done. A very similar use of supports had existed in sculpture for centuries, as for example, on the well-known relief with the *Adoration of the Magi* at Cividale.[8] Perhaps it is not an accident that the wheel-like supports are found on only one capital at Autun, that of the *Flight into Egypt*. Here, the added influence could have come from the wooden figures of donkeys on wheels carrying Christ in processions on Palm Sundays.[9] The sculptor of the capital at Saulieu, who imitated the composition of the Autun capital, certainly interpreted these ornaments as wheels, for he used only four of them, one under each of the donkey's hoofs [pl. ⓓ10].

PRESENTATION OF THE CHURCH [pl. 13].

The original of this capital is in the 'Salle Capitulaire' and has been replaced by a copy. Its situation on the north-

---

[1] II, 11.

[2] G. Vezin, *L'adoration et le cycle des Mages dans l'art chrétien primitif*, Paris, 1950, pp. 21-23.

[3] A similar box is held by one of the Magi or the servant on the south tympanum at Vézelay (Salet, *op. cit.*, p. 180, pl. 24).

[4] *Matthew*, II, 12.

[5] *Matthew*, II, 13-14.

[6] A sword of exactly the same shape is used by Abraham in the *Sacrifice of Isaac* [pl. 39].

[7] There is much likelihood that there was another capital with a row of rosettes above the necking. Two of these rosettes are now attached to the *Presentation of the Church* in the 'Salle Capitulaire', but they did not belong to it originally. At least, they do not appear on the copy of that capital on the north-west pier of the crossing but under the copy of the *Adoration of the Magi*.

[8] G. Marioni and C. Mutinelli, *Guida storico-artistica di Cividale*, Udine, 1958, fig. 136.

[9] That such figures existed in the 12th century is proved by the still surviving example in Zurich (F. Gysin, *Holtzplastik vom 11. bis zum 14. Jahrhundert*, Berne, 1958, p. 13, pls. 4 and 5).

west pier of the crossing makes it immediately visible to anyone entering the cathedral by the north doorway, originally the principal entrance to the church.

On the main side of the capital are two figures: a layman[1] and a bishop with a staff, who between them hold a model of a church. Above them, the heavens open and from the clouds emerge the head and the right arm of a young figure.

A. Kingsley Porter suggested that this scene represents the Duke Hugh II presenting the cathedral to St. Lazarus.[2] Unfortunately, Gislebertus did not give a nimbus to any of the figures in this scene, and his omission makes the task of identification extremely difficult. Kingsley Porter may be right in seeing in the young figure Duke Hugh II, who gave the land on which the new church was erected and who, no doubt, also contributed funds for the building. It is very likely that the canons of Autun wanted to express their gratitude to the Duke and perhaps also to flatter him in this way. But is not the figure facing the Duke their own Bishop, Étienne de Bâgé? Had the figure of the bishop been St. Lazarus, as bishop of Marseilles, there would have been no need to carve yet another figure in heaven. If, however, the two figures holding the model of the church are Duke Hugh and Bishop Étienne, then the person appearing from the clouds is perhaps St. Lazarus, or even Christ.

An interesting point is that the model of the church consists of the apse, the transept, and the crossing tower (now partly broken off). It is very tempting to see in this a deliberate attempt to show the church approximately as it looked when the capital was carved. It should be remembered that the capital was on the pier of the crossing, and that, when it was carved, the work on the transept and the crossing was in progress, though the nave was certainly not yet far advanced.

On the well-known 12th-century altar at Avenas (Rhône)[3] there is a relief showing a 'King Louis' offering the church to St. Vincent [pl. Ⓑ10].[4] There the church is very similar indeed to that on our capital but in addition to the apse, transept and crossing tower, it also has the nave. St. Vincent, shown with a nimbus, does not carry the church but makes a gesture of acceptance.

To the left of the main scene on our capital is a curving branch of foliage with a nude putto eating fruit and a bird looking like a parrot. These are purely decorative motifs. The putto is clearly derived from the antique and the imitation goes so far even that small drilled holes are used in representing the hair in the antique manner. On the opposite side, two figures were carved. One is broken off, except for the feet; it seems to have been

facing the other, a youth with a diadem, asleep on a throne. This may be some reference to a dream connected with the foundation of the church of St. Lazarus but for lack of any documentary information on the subject, this can only remain a tentative suggestion.

The figure of the bishop on this capital is extremely close, in the treatment of the folds, to the angel from the arch of the north doorway. The similarity is so striking that one must assume that both were carved within a very short space of time. (See pl. VII and p. 146.)

GOD SPEAKING TO CAIN [pl. 14]. The capital on the south-western pier of the crossing, facing south, was identified by Abbé Terret as the 'Betrayal of Judas'.[4] This is certainly wrong. The scene represents God the Father asking Cain: 'Where is Abel thy brother?'[5] Cain stands defiantly with one hand on his hip and a club in the other. Behind him, round the angle of the capital, the body of Abel lies hidden in the foliage. In contrast to God and Cain, Abel's eyes have no drilled pupils, for they are closed; his body is also nude: Gislebertus often used one or other, or both of these conventions to show that a figure is dead, dying or suffering (cf., the *Death of Cain* [pl. 18], where Cain is clothed, while his eyes are shut, *St. Vincent* [pl. 41], the *Stoning of St. Stephen* [pl. 25], the *Suicide of Judas* [pl. 17], the *Three Hebrews in the Fiery Furnace* [pl. 36], *Lazarus* [pl. II]).

This capital is one of the few in the cathedral carved in thick-grained stone. Consequently, the sculpture lacks the crispness and fine finish which are so characteristic of Gislebertus's work.

THE ANNUNCIATION TO ST. JOSEPH [pl. 47]. All the capitals of the nave which have been discussed so far are placed low, at the level of the springing of the nave arcades. The capitals of the great pilasters are carved with foliage or grotesque motifs, except for this capital and the *Ball-Players* [pl. 46].

Gislebertus based his carving on the text of St. Matthew, which reads: 'Now the birth of Jesus Christ was on this wise: When as his mother Mary was espoused to Joseph, before they came together, she was found with child of the Holy Ghost. Then Joseph her husband, being a just man, and not willing to make her a public example, was minded to put her away privily. But while he thought of these things, behold, the angel of the Lord appeared unto him in a dream, saying, Joseph, thou son of David, fear not to take unto thee Mary thy wife; for that which is conceived in her is of the Holy Ghost.'[6]

Thus the scene here described is, in fact, the *Annunciation to St. Joseph* and it is this subject that is carved on our capital. The angel is shown facing Joseph and holding his hand while pointing to Mary, seated behind with the dove of the Holy Ghost above her.

[1] A fragment in the possession of Miss A. Oppé, London, shows a striking similarity to this figure. See pl. Ⓑ11, and Appendix 2, p. 178.
[2] A. K. Porter, *Romanesque Sculpture of the Pilgrimage Roads*, Boston, 1923, vol. I, p. 113.
[3] P. Deschamps, *French Sculpture of the Romanesque period. Eleventh and Twelfth Centuries*, Florence-Paris, 1930, pl. 51B.
[4] On stylistic grounds it is impossible to accept the identification of Rex Ludovicus as Louis VII as suggested by Ch. Perrat, *L'autel d'Avenas, la légende de Ganelon et les expéditions de Louis VII en Bourgogne (1166-72)*, Lyons, 1932.

[4] Terret, *Autun II*, p. 17.
[5] *Genesis*, IV, 9.
[6] I, 18-20.

Why should this narrative capital be placed so high up, where it can hardly be seen? The answer seems to be that Gislebertus wanted to relate it as closely as possible to another capital, which is immediately below it, on the west face of the second pier, and which represents the *Tree of Jesse*.

THE TREE OF JESSE [pl. 15]. The opening verses of the first chapter of St. Matthew, immediately preceding the description of St. Joseph's dream, enumerate the ancestors of Christ, from Abraham to Joseph, the husband of Mary. In this list of ancestors, the name of King David is particularly stressed to show that Jesus was, through Joseph, of royal descent. The capital which will now be described seems to be connected with this passage as well as with the prophecy of Isaiah:[1] *Et egredietur virga de radice Iesse, et flos de radice eius ascendet* ('And there shall come forth a shoot out of Jesse, and a branch out of his roots shall bear fruit'). The similarity of the sound between *virga* (shoot) and *virgo* (virgin) resulted in an early association of this prophecy with the Virgin Mary, while the word *flos* (fruit, or, more exactly, flower) was invariably interpreted to mean Christ.[2]

Isaiah's prophecy inspired the artists of the Romanesque period to evolve a visual form for it, known as the *Tree of Jesse*. Before the iconography of this subject was given its final form in about the middle of the 12th century, various experiments were made, chiefly in manuscript illumination. In these experiments, Burgundy played a very important part.[3]

The composition of the *Tree of Jesse* on our capital consists of a central vertical stem with a fruit at the top, while within the curving branches of foliage on either side sits a king on a throne holding fruit which grows from the branch. The kings are probably David, the son of Jesse, and Solomon.[4] Thus Christ's genealogy is represented here in an allegorical form; and the words of the angel: 'Joseph, thou son of David', in the *Annunciation* scene [pl. 47], are fully supported in visual form by this image of Joseph's royal ancestors just below.

This Autun capital was copied crudely in the 12th century at Beaune [pl. ①3]. At Vézelay, a capital of the narthex is carved with a somewhat similar composition that is of purely decorative character.[5]

THE DREAM OF NEBUCHADNEZZAR [pl. 16]. The subject of the capital on the west face of the sixth pier, on the south side of the nave, has never been satisfactorily explained.[6]

The capital represents a tree that is unique among the sculpture at Autun, for no other plant form there symbolises a tree so well: it has a high trunk with branches growing out of it, each ending in a large fruit. Below, a figure lies on his back holding an axe or a pick, aiming a blow with it at the tree. Above the tree, with his feet hidden behind one of its branches, is the figure of a pilgrim, recognisable by his scrip and characteristic staff. The two pilgrims on the lintel of the west doorway have the same attributes [pl. Q]; and Christ in the scene of the *Journey to Emmaus* [pl. 2] also has a scrip and staff in this form. The explanation of this mysterious subject is perhaps found in the *Book of Daniel*, in the description of the *Dream of Nebuchadnezzar* successfully interpreted by Daniel.[7]

'I saw, and behold a tree in the midst of the earth, and the height thereof was great . . . I saw in the visions of my head upon my bed and, behold, a watcher and an holy one came down from heaven. He cried aloud, and said thus; Hew down the tree, and cut off his branches...'

If we could be certain that the pilgrim is 'an holy one' of the dream, then the identification proposed here could be accepted as correct, for the pose of the man with the axe agrees well with his being asleep.

That the *Dream of Nebuchadnezzar* was illustrated by Romanesque sculptors is proved by a relief on the doorway at Ripoll in Catalonia.[8] But there, it has quite a different form from the representation at Autun. On the other hand, an illumination in the *Liber Floridus* of Lambert, a canon of St. Omer, finished before 1120, now in Ghent University Library (Cod. 1125), has on folio 232 v° the *Dream of Nebuchadnezzar*, which has certain common motives with the Autun capital. The Babylonian king is lying asleep under the tree. He is shown the second time with an axe cutting the tree. Above the tree is Christ in majesty with a sword and ordering with the gesture of his left hand the tree to be cut down.

Although the interpretation of this capital as the *Dream of Nebuchadnezzar* is inconclusive, perhaps it is not without significance that one of the capitals on the corresponding sixth pier on the north side of the nave, the *Three Hebrews in the Fiery Furnace*, is also an illustration of the *Book of Daniel*. In several instances it has been obvious that the capitals of the corresponding piers on both sides of the choir and nave were carved within a short space of time of each other and that often they are related in their subject or source.

THE DEATH OF CAIN [pl. 18]. The second episode in the story of Cain was placed on the north side of the

---

[1] XI, 1.

[2] A. Watson, *The Early Iconography of the Tree of Jesse*, Oxford-London, 1934, pp. 2-3.

[3] Watson, *op. cit.*, quotes four early representations of the *Tree of Jesse* made in Burgundy, pls. III, V, VI and X. Of these the most significant from our point of view is that in the Bible of Saint Benignus (Dijon, Bibl. Mun., MS. 2, fol. 406 r°) for it is found at the beginning of St. Matthew's Gospel.

[4] A similar composition—two men, one of whom is crowned, within the branches of the *Tree of Jesse* and holding the fruit growing on these branches—is found on a leaf from a *Speculum Virginum* in Bonn (Watson, *op. cit.*, pl. XXX). David and Solomon occur frequently on the *Tree of Jesse* (Watson, *op. cit.*, for instance, on pls. XXII and XXIII).

[5] Salet, *op. cit.*, pl. 44.

[6] Abbé Devoucoux (*op. cit.*, p. 47) described the capital as a fight between two men, one armed with the *ascia* or double-edged axe, the other with the *pistillus* or iron rod; the *ascia* being a symbol analogous with the wolf, the *pistillus* with that of the lion. Abbé Terret, on the other hand, suggested (*Autun*, II, p. 7) that the capital illustrates Psalm XXXVI, verses 35-36.

[7] IV, 10-17.

[8] Porter, *op. cit.*, illustr. 576.

nave, on the second pier (the original capital is today in the 'Salle Capitulaire'). This capital and *God Speaking to Cain* are both in thick-grained stone. It is obvious that they were carved in quick succession, not only because of the connection between their subjects but also because their design and especially the foliage backgrounds are so similar.

Although the killing of Cain by Lamech is implied in *Genesis*,[1] the full story is told in the apocrypha of the Old Testament.[2] Lamech, in spite of his blindness in old age (he lived 777 years according to the Bible), liked to go hunting, guided by his son Tubalcain. The latter mistook Cain for a wild animal hiding in the bushes and directed Lamech's arrow at him.

This episode was probably transmitted to Romanesque art from Byzantine sources[3] and enjoyed a wide popularity.[4] At Vézelay this subject was carved twice on two separate capitals.[5] At both Autun and Vézelay, Cain has horns on his head, a detail which resulted from a strange interpretation of the following passage in Genesis, 'And the Lord set a mark upon Cain, lest any finding him should kill him'.[6]

The Autun *Death of Cain* is full of drama and more subtle than the same subject at Vézelay. Lamech discharges his arrow smiling, for he enjoys his hunting. Tubalcain directs the blind man's left arm (Lamech is shown left-handed) and points towards Cain. Cain, enclosed by large acanthus leaves to show that he is hiding in the woods, has one arrow in his throat and a horrible expression of agony on his face. His hands, helplessly crossed, and the whole position of his body show a close analogy with the body of Goliath [pl. 54] on the capital of the north doorway of the west façade. No Byzantine illuminations, mosaics or other Romanesque carvings with this scene, contain so much dramatic tension.

As on many other Autun capitals, the eyes of the participants, except for the dead man's, have drilled pupils.

THE SUICIDE OF JUDAS [pl. 17]. We shall now examine the first of the two historiated capitals on the south wall. This depicts the *Suicide of Judas*.[7] The capital faces *God Speaking to Cain* [pl. 14] and was, no doubt, carved shortly after it and the *Death of Cain* [pl. 18]. It is easy to imagine that the *Suicide of Judas* was conceived as a New Testament counterpart to the *Death of Cain*. In both cases their terrible guilt leads each finally to a violent death.

The naked body of Judas hangs on a rope attached to a tree. On either side of the corpse winged devils, with fearful grimaces on their faces, pull the rope down. A round object attached to the rope probably symbolises the purse containing the thirty pieces of silver. Two branches of foliage form graceful curves in imitation of the angle volutes of a Corinthian capital. The scene is strictly symmetrical, but is charged with drama. The wide-open mouth of Judas expresses despair and at the same time makes his face akin to those of the two devils beside him.

The Autun capital was copied at Saulieu, but there the scene lacks any of the dramatic qualities of its model [pl. Ⓓ9].[8] The same subject is found also at Vézelay.[9]

TWO VIRTUES AND TWO VICES [pl. 19]. On the east face of the second pier of the south nave arcade, is a capital which is closely connected with the previous two. Judas was led to his doom by greed and Cain by anger ('And the Lord said, Why art thou wroth?'[10]). These two Vices, *Avaritia* and *Ira*, are carved at the bottom of the capital, the first with a purse, the other piercing itself with a sword.[11] Standing on the heads of the Vices, and thus proclaiming their victory, are two Virtues: *Largitas*, with a chalice, and *Patientia*.

It has already been said that the idea of the struggle of the Virtues and Vices is derived from Prudentius' *Psychomachia*. But in this particular case, there is a deliberate selection of a pair of Virtues and Vices, to illustrate the moral shortcomings of Cain and Judas whose stories were told on the previous capitals. From this example, it will be seen how much thought went into the choice of subjects of some of the Autun capitals.

On the capital of the *Suicide of Judas*, the foliage was arranged to serve the function of the angle volutes. In this case, the heads of the two Virtues are placed at the angles and so the foliage curves inwards, making the composition once again wonderfully balanced.

NOAH'S ARK [pl. 20]. *Noah's Ark* was one of the favourite subjects in Romanesque art. Some artists devoted considerable attention to it, representing several episodes of the story of the Flood.[12] For instance, on the frieze of Lincoln Cathedral there are no less than six scenes.[13]

---

[1] IV, 15 and 23.

[2] *Reallexikon zur deutschen Kunstgeschichte*, vol. I, 1937, p. 22.

[3] Cf. for instance the *Octateuch* in the Vatican (Gr. 747).

[4] The most spectacular are the scenes on the frieze at Modena (Salvini, *op. cit.*, pl. 45) and amongst the mosaics at Monreale (O. Demus, *The Mosaics of Norman Sicily*, London, 1949, pl. 99A). See also G. Zarnecki, *Later English Romanesque Sculpture 1140-1210*, London, 1953, p. 24.

[5] Salet, *op. cit.*, pls. 37 and 44.

[6] IV, 15.

[7] *Matthew*, XXVII, 5. The most recent study of the subject is by O. Goetz, *Hie henckt Judas*, in *Form und Inhalt*, Stuttgart, 1950.

[8] At Saulieu, the purse has been repeated but more as a decorative embellishment, with beading.

[9] Salet, *op. cit.*, pl. 31. The Vézelay carving shows some resemblance to the *Suicide of Judas* in the *Psalter of St. Bertin* (Boulogne-sur-Mer, Bibl. Mun., MS. 20) decorated in 999 by Otbert, abbot of the abbey.

[10] *Genesis*, IV, 6.

[11] The same subject of the *Suicide of Ira* is found on one of the capitals in the main apse [pl. Ⓐ1]. Notice that *Ira* is nude while *Avaritia* is fully clothed in accordance with Gislebertus's convention for representing dead or dying figures.

[12] *Genesis*, VI, 13-IX, 17.

[13] F. Saxl, *English Sculptures of the Twelfth Century*, London, 1954, pls. XXXVII-XLIII.

At Autun, there is only one scene connected with Noah, a carving showing the loading of the ark. Abbé Terret[1] assumed that it was the unloading, since the ark rests on a mountain formed by small leaves, presumably Mount Ararat, mentioned in *Genesis*. But on the other hand Noah, who is on the extreme left, has an axe in his belt; he has, therefore, just finished building the ark.

The ark is in the form of a timber house, with two storeys marked by round windows. In the lower window can be seen two animals, in the upper, the head of a woman. Noah hands a child to a figure already inside the ark, while on the right-hand side two men load a sack, presumably of food.

At Vézelay,[2] the Noah story is also represented by one episode, the *Building of the Ark*, in which the ark is of a very similar construction to that at Autun. At Beaune, the ark is even closer in form to Autun but the carving is rather crude. Although the Beaune capital seems to have been modelled on that of Gislebertus, it shows the ark floating on the water with Noah leaning out and praying [pl. ①2].

CHRIST'S APPEARANCE TO ST. MARY MAG-DALEN [pl. 21].

The capital on the west side of the third pier of the north nave arcade is carved with three episodes illustrating Christ's appearance to Mary Magdalen after his resurrection. On the right face of the capital, three women (the head of one is missing) are on their way to anoint the body of Christ. They discover the tomb empty and an angel seated on top of the sepulchre. Frightened, they run away[3] and two of them are shown again on the opposite side discussing their experience. In the centre, Christ is appearing to Mary Magdalen who, still with a bottle of spices in her hand, kneels to embrace his feet. Christ leans back, his arms raised, to illustrate the words: *Noli me tangere* ('Touch me not').[4]

Eight figures are carved on this capital and, in addition, four branches of foliage, each curving like volutes. Yet there is no overcrowding; the narrative is perfectly clear and the gestures natural. The remarkable gifts of Gislebertus can best be seen when comparing his works with sculptures derived from them. A capital at Saulieu representing the *Noli me tangere* scene is a replica of that at Autun [pl. ①8] and though the sculpture is competent, it lacks the depth of feeling and the expressive form of Gislebertus's masterpiece.

SAMSON BRINGING DOWN THE TEMPLE [pl. 22].

The vengeance and death of Samson, as described in the *Book of Judges*,[5] is a story full of drama and is not easy to transmit into a carving restricted by the peculiar form

of a capital. Unfortunately, the carving at Autun is damaged but in spite of this, the ingenuity and originality of Gislebertus can well be appreciated.

The composition consists of two episodes, both set against a background of rich foliage. On the left, Samson, betrayed by Delilah and blinded by the Philistines, is being led by a boy from the prison to the temple of Dagon, to amuse the gathered crowd of the Philistines. The upper part of Samson's body is broken off.

'Now the house was full of men and women; and all the lords of the Philistines were there; and there were upon the roof about three thousand men and women, that beheld while Samson made sport.' The temple on the capital is only a symbol, an artistic shorthand. It is a tiny structure with round arches through which a few heads of men and women look out. The Bible says specifically that Samson 'took hold of the two middle pillars upon which the house stood . . . and the house fell upon the lords, and upon all the people that were therein.' Gislebertus carved only one pillar and showed Samson embracing it in his last effort to avenge his blindness by pulling down the temple filled with his enemies, and finding death himself under the ruins. It is left to the onlookers to imagine the second pillar hidden in the body of the capital.

Although it was more usual to represent Samson between two columns, as for instance in the Byzantine *Octateuchs*, (for example, in the Vatican Gr. 747), or on the 12th-century capital from Notre-Dame-des-Doms, Avignon, now in the Fogg Museum,[6] occasionally artists did not follow the Bible too closely, and represented Samson pulling down one pillar only as in the *Psalter of St. Bertin* in the Bibliothèque Municipale at Boulogne-sur-Mer (MS. 20, fol. 63 v°), and on the doorway at Nivelles in Belgium.[7]

COCKFIGHT [pl. 23].

So overwhelming a majority of the Autun capitals are decorated with sculpture of a religious or moral character that, when examining an obviously secular subject, there is a tendency to become suspicious and try to find in it some hidden allegory. Abbé Terret realised that this capital was derived from an antique model, but was convinced that it had a moral significance all the same.[8]

The carving represents two cocks of which one is clearly about to win the fight. Behind each cock stands a nude spectator: the one behind the winning cock beams with joy, while the other expresses his disappointment by an angry grimace and raised fists.

M. Jean Adhémar, in discussing this capital, writes 'The squat forms, the voluminous modelling of the bodies, the expressions of the faces, confirm the hypothesis suggested by iconography; this is not a scene which the

[1] Terret, *Autun*, II, p. 15.
[2] Salet, *op. cit.*, pl. 28.
[3] *Mark*, XVI, 1-10.
[4] *John*, XX, 17.
[5] XIII, 1-18.

[6] Deschamps, *op. cit.*, pl. 85c.
[7] L. Tollenaere, *La sculpture sur pierre de l'ancien diocèse de Liège à l'époque romane*, Gembloux, 1957, pl. xxvb.
[8] Abbé Terret saw in this capital an illustration of the second Epistle of St. Paul to Timothy (II, 5) *Autun*, II, p. 56.

sculptor had seen and reproduced; without any doubt, he copied a sarcophagus.'[1]

This Autun capital was imitated at Saulieu, but there the composition is in reverse [pl. Ⓓ11].

THE STONING OF ST. STEPHEN [pl. 25]. This is on the west face of the third pier on the south side. The subject is based on the *Acts of the Apostles* describing the stoning of Stephen, the first deacon and proto-martyr.[2]

On either side of the saint are three Jews. Each of the two next to him has a stone raised in his right hand ready to throw, and with his left carries a further supply of stones in the folds of his cloak. Three other perse-cutors also throw stones, one of them with both hands, to give his blow more force. The figure on the extreme right approaches with a club. On the left side of the capital, a man is seated and his gestures suggest that he is giving orders. He was rightly identified by Abbé Terret[3] as Saul, the future St. Paul, who witnessed the stoning of St. Stephen and 'was consenting unto his death'.[4]

St. Stephen is in the centre of the main face of the capital, nude, in an attitude of prayer. Three stones form a kind of nimbus or crown around his head.[5] Above him, Christ appears from the clouds, blessing the martyr.[6]

Except for Saul under whose feet is an arcaded sup-port, all the other figures in this scene are standing on scrolls of foliage of a type not found on other capitals at Autun—thin bands forming small volutes.

The popularity of the cult of St. Stephen was very great during the Middle Ages and his martyrdom was frequently represented in 12th-century sculpture: for instance, the Moissac cloister, the Cahors tympanum, the Montsaunés doorway, the Chambon lintel, the St. Pons capital and the Vermenton doorway.[7]

The Autun capital, like so many others, was copied at Beaune [pl. Ⓓ1]. The copyist increased the number of figures and introduced a few new motives not without naïve charm, but entirely lacking in the dramatic feeling of Gislebertus's work.

JACOB WRESTLING WITH THE ANGEL [pl. 26]. The capital on the east side of the trumeau supporting the lintel of the central doorway is decorated with three episodes from the story of Jacob. On the left side Jacob flees to Padan-aram in Mesopotamia after having de-prived his brother Esau of his birthright.[8] He is re-presented here in a very similar way to Joachim fleeing to the mountains in the *Annunciation to St. Anne* [pl. 37],

carrying his belongings on a stick over his left shoulder. On the right side of the capital, Jacob at Bethel, after having seen a vision of the ladder and having been blessed, takes the stone he used as a pillow and sets it up as a pillar.[9]

On the main face of the capital, Jacob is wrestling with the angel.[10] This theme, so popular in Romanesque art, is used twice at Vézelay.[11]

The story of Jacob was fully illustrated in the Greek *Octateuchs* and they must have served as the chief source for Gislebertus. For instance, in the *Octateuch* in the Vatican (Gr. 747), all three scenes carved on this capital are found.

DANIEL IN THE LIONS' DEN [pl. 27]. Two of the capitals of the nave are devoted to subjects from the Old Testament, showing how the people who refused to abandon their faith were thrown to their deaths, but were miraculously saved by God's intervention. The story of Daniel cast into the den of lions by Darius is told in the *Book of Daniel*[12] but it is augmented in the apocryphal *History of the Destruction of Bel and the Dragon* by the episode of Habbacuc.[13]

Gislebertus illustrated this apocryphal story. Daniel sits under an arch which is a convention frequently used in depicting caves. Two ferocious lions on either side keep their distance from him. Habbacuc, who was on his way to the fields carrying food for his reapers, is being brought to Daniel; he is suspended in mid-air, a flying angel holding him by the hair.

The second capital with a related subject is found further west in the nave, on the east face of the sixth pier. It is:

THREE HEBREWS IN THE FIERY FURNACE [pl. 36]. This capital illustrates the story, also from the *Book of Daniel*, of the three Jews set by Nebuchad-nezzar over the province of Babylon who refused to wor-ship the golden image and in punishment were cast into a fiery furnace; but they were protected by an angel and thus came out unharmed.[14]

The furnace is indicated by an arch and flames. The three Jews, nude and in an attitude of prayer, are being covered with a cloak by a flying angel.

The two servants who cast the three Jews into the furnace stand one on either side of the arch. The *Book of Daniel* tells us that they perished from heat and, indeed, both figures raise their hands to their foreheads as if to wipe away the sweat. The figure on the left, with a club, is dressed in a short tunic but the other is nude—a sign of suffering or death.

Above the furnace there is a row of palmette-like leaves and below a pattern of beading.

[1] Adhémar, *op. cit.*, p. 162.
[2] VII, 54-60.
[3] Terret, *Autun*, II, p. 11.
[4] *Acts*, VIII, 1.
[5] Abbé Terret quotes the words of Gregory of Nyssa referring to the stones around St. Stephen's head as forming a crown (*op. cit.*, p. 11, n. 9).
[6] Compare a similar motif on the capital, *Presentation of the Church*, where however, the figure is more likely to be Lazarus and not Christ.
[7] Porter, *op. cit.*, pls. 275, 426, 506, 1250, 1272, 1498.
[8] *Genesis*, XXVIII, 5.

[9] *Ibid.*, XXVIII, 18.
[10] *Ibid.*, XXXII, 24-30.
[11] Salet, *op. cit.*, pls. 40 and 43.
[12] VI.
[13] Verses 33-39.
[14] III.

The carving on this capital was not completed, for one of the flowers has not the same fine finish as the rest and also the arch of the furnace is plain, without any moulding, which is most unusual. Probably it was urgently needed and there was no time to give it the finish which is found in Gislebertus's other works.

THE SECOND TEMPTATION OF CHRIST [pl. 28]. Both St. Matthew and St. Luke describe how, after having fasted for forty days in the wilderness, Jesus was tempted by the devil. He first suggested that Jesus could change stones into bread, which was the subject of Gislebertus's capital in the choir [pl. 3]. Then he took Christ to Jerusalem and set him on a pinnacle of the temple and said, 'If thou be the Son of God, cast thyself down'.[1]

It is this passage from the Gospels that Gislebertus illustrated on the capital of the west face of the fourth pier, on the north side of the nave. Strangely enough, it is the devil only who stands on the top of the temple. Christ, with the angel on guard behind him, sits facing the devil. The gestures and the expressions of all the participants are extraordinarily vivid. The cunning of the devil, the unperturbed dignity of Christ, the hasty reaction of the angel, who raises a sword in readiness, tell the story better than any words.

The fact that Gislebertus carved two of the *Temptations of Christ* [pls. 3 and 28] is not surprising, nor was it an isolated case. In the *Psalter of St. Bertin*,[2] for instance, there are three representations of the subject corresponding to the three temptations described in the Gospels.

SAMSON AND THE LION [pl. 29]. On the east face of the fourth pier of the south arcade is carved one of the favourite subjects of Romanesque sculpture, *Samson and the Lion*. Samson, unarmed, sits astride a lion and breaks its jaws with his bare hands.[3] This exploit of courage and strength had an obvious appeal. Moreover, various allegorical meanings were attached to Samson's triumph over the lion,[4] thus adding to the popularity of this subject. Under the lion's left front paw is a head, possibly that of its victim. Behind Samson, in the foliage, is a small nude figure with an expression of terror on its face, probably someone seeking safety from the lion in a tree.

This capital, together with the one on the other side of the same pier, raises an important problem of style, which it will be more convenient to discuss after describing the next capital.

CHRIST WASHING THE APOSTLES' FEET[5] [pl. 31]. One of the apostles is seated on a richly carved chair. In front of him Christ, with a cruciform nimbus, washes his feet in a basin. Two other apostles are behind Christ, one with a towel, the other taking off his shoes.

This and the previous capital, both on the fourth pier, show a style quite different from that of the other capitals of the nave. Undoubtedly, not all the sculptures were carved entirely by Gislebertus; many of the foliage capitals in particular were probably only designed by him, and the work carried out by his assistants under his supervision. But the fact that a few capitals were left unfinished shows that Gislebertus did not like to entrust any figure sculpture to his collaborators.

However, the two capitals in question are clearly not by him. It is significant that both capitals are on one pier which suggests that for some reason Gislebertus was not available at the time when this pier was being erected. It is possible that one of his assistants executed the work, using drawings from the workshop's pattern book. But though there are general stylistic similarities with Gislebertus's figure style—for example, similar facial types, similar draperies and a similar relation of figures to the foliage background—at the same time the figures are shorter and bulkier, the poses and gestures less lively, almost frozen in their immobility, the foliage of quite a different design and far more repetitive than in Gislebertus's work. It is most tempting, as has already been suggested, to attribute the two capitals under discussion to the author of the capitals that are now in the Fogg Museum in Cambridge (U.S.A.).[6] The similarity of the Autun capital representing the *Journey to Emmaus* to the capital with the same subject at Moûtiers-Saint-Jean has been discussed earlier. There can be no doubt at all that the Moûtiers-Saint-Jean master had an intimate knowledge of the Autun sculptures. Some of the foliage capitals from Moûtiers-Saint-Jean are strikingly similar to those at Autun. One of them in particular[7] shows a strikingly similar modelling to the foliage forming the background of *Christ Washing the Apostles' Feet*. On another capital at Moûtiers-Saint-Jean is a damaged *Samson and the Lion* [pl. ⓑ5] and though it is in a reversed position to the same scene at Autun, their close relationship is obvious.

In the chapters dealing with the style and influence of the Autun sculptures, the connection between Autun and Moûtiers-Saint-Jean will be discussed further.

MOSES AND THE GOLDEN CALF [pl. 30]. On the south wall of the south aisle facing the fourth pier is a capital illustrating Moses' destruction of the golden idol set up by the Jews while he was on Mount Sinai.[8] Moses, the tables in one hand, strikes the golden calf with a staff. Behind the calf is a winged devil with flame-like hair bound with ribbon. His fearful face is distorted by anger on seeing the work of his inspiration being destroyed.

[1] *Matthew*, IV, 6; *Luke*, IV, 9.
[2] Boulogne-sur-Mer, Bibl. Mun., MS. 20.
[3] *Judges*, XIV, 5-6.
[4] K. Kunstle, *Ikonographie der christlichen Kunst*, Freiburg im Breisgau, 1928, vol. I, pp. 297 *seq.* Samson symbolised Christ, and the lion, the devil.
[5] *John*, XIII, 4-5.

[6] A. K. Porter, *Romanesque Capitals*, in *Fogg Art Museum Notes*, Cambridge (U.S.A.), 1932, figs. 1-16.
[7] Porter, *op. cit.*, fig. 13.
[8] *Exodus*, XXXII, 19-20.

This appears to be one of the capitals in the west end of the nave that were left unfinished.

The same subject is found carved at Vézelay,[1] where, though the scene differs in having more figures, the composition is very similar. Perhaps both capitals derive from a lost prototype at Cluny. What can only be a guess in this case is a certainty with the *Fourth Tone of Music*, which will be discussed shortly.

THE CONVERSION OF ST. PAUL [pl. 32]. The capital on the north face of the fifth pier of the north arcade has hitherto been considered as representing the 'Healing of the Man Blind from Birth in the Pool of Siloam'.[2] But this identification is certainly wrong. The scene on the capital is based on the description of the conversion of St. Paul in the *Acts of the Apostles*.[3] Paul, or rather Saul, as he was then called, the great persecutor of the Christians, was on his way to Damascus when Christ called to him, 'Saul, Saul, why persecutest thou me?' Saul is shown half-bald, as he usually is in art, with knees bent to suggest that he is lying on the ground (it is, for instance, in such a pose that Goliath's body is carved on a capital of the façade [pl. 54]). Saul's crossed hands show his submission to Christ who stands in front of him with one hand raised, addressing him. Behind is an angel, so often found assisting Christ in Gislebertus's sculptures.

To the left is the culminating episode of the story. Saul, blind since his vision, was lead to Damascus. He remained blind for three days, until a disciple called Ananias came to him and said: 'Brother Saul, the Lord, even Jesus, that appeared unto thee in the way as thou camest, hath sent me, that thou mightest receive thy sight, and be filled with the Holy Ghost. And immediately there fell from his eyes as it had been scales; and he received sight forthwith, and arose, and was baptised.'

Ananias is seen standing on the left with a book and blessing Paul, who is immersed in an improvised font, made from a barrel. He is the same half-bald figure to whom Christ speaks on the main side of the capital. But here, as he is receiving baptism, and in anticipation, so to speak, of his subsequent life, Gislebertus carved a nimbus round his head.

The *Conversion of St. Paul* is certainly unfinished; on the surface of the background are the visible marks of the claw-chisel, which on practically all other capitals were removed by the final polish.

This capital makes a very suitable complement to the following scene.

ST. PETER IN CHAINS [pl. 33]. The capital on the west side of the same pier illustrates two episodes from the story of the deliverance of St. Peter from prison.[4] The action of the story took place indoors and so three sides of the capital are enclosed by arches with the turrets at angles. The space under the central arcade represents the interior of the prison, while the side arches show its exterior walls. The place was well guarded—'and the keepers before the door kept the prison'. Indeed, under the right arcade, there is a door firmly bolted and a guard armed with a club stands on the doorstep holding the key. Below are waves of water, obviously representing a defensive moat.

Under the main arcade St. Peter sits 'bound with two chains', one round his neck and the other round his ankles. In front of him an angel points through the arcade the way to freedom.

The next episode is shown under the left arcade. The angel leads St. Peter out of prison and makes a sign to him to go. St. Peter is shown here as a dignified figure once more, in ecclesiastical vestments and holding a book.

The arcades of the prison, their capitals and the columns are carved with minute foliage motifs and other enrichments of great delicacy. The same subject is twice repeated at Vézelay but there it is treated quite differently.[5]

THE FOURTH TONE OF MUSIC [pl. 34]. The east capital of the fifth pier on the south side, once identified by Abbé Terret as the 'Good Shepherd'[6] represents the *Fourth Tone of Music* and is a free copy of one of the ambulatory capitals at Cluny [pl. Ⓑ17].[7] On two of these capitals are carved the eight tones of Gregorian plainsong. The fourth tone is symbolised by a musician ringing bells suspended from a rod, which he carries on his shoulder and over which he puts one arm. At Vézelay, a fairly faithful copy of this is found on a capital of the north doorway.[8] Gislebertus reversed the position of the musician on his capital and added two assistants, who sit on either side. There are four bells suspended from the rod, and two more are held by the standing figure. A bell is also fixed to the hem of his tunic. One of the seated musicians holds a bell in one hand and a hammer in another.

Why Gislebertus selected only one out of eight tones of plainsong is difficult to understand. The sophisticated scheme found at Cluny was perhaps of no particular interest to him and he took only one subject because of its decorative value, enriched it with additional figures and details and included it in his capital, in spite of the fact that his decorative scheme consisted of predominantly narrative religious subjects.

The narrow sides of the capital are filled with foliage, while the abacus is carved with a geometric pattern identical with that decorating the mandorla of the west tympanum.

[1] Salet, *op. cit.*, pl. 40.
[2] Terret, *Autun*, II, p. 31. The miracle is described in *John*, IX.
[3] IX, 1-18.
[4] XII, 1-10.

[5] Salet, *op. cit.*, pl. 40.
[6] Terret, *Autun*, II, p. 11.
[7] Deschamps, *op. cit.*, pl. 44. Dr. Joan Evans discusses the relation of the Cluny capitals with illuminated MSS. in *Cluniac Art of the Romanesque Period*, Cambridge, 1950, pp. 116 *seq.*
[8] Salet, *op. cit.*, pl. 25.

THE ASCENT OF SIMON MAGUS [pl. 35]. The only information about Simon Magus contained in the New Testament is that he was a sorcerer of Samaria who, after having been baptised, offered money to St. Peter to obtain spiritual powers from him (hence the term 'simony'). For this he was severely reprimanded.[1]

According to later writers[2] Simon came into conflict with St. Peter and St. Paul in Rome. With the help of a devil, he was able to fly in the air but the apostles' prayer deprived him of this magic power and he crashed to the ground and was killed.

The legend is illustrated on two capitals, facing each other. The first episode shows Simon with wings attached to his arms and legs flying up over two branches of foliage, probably representing trees. St. Peter, with his key in his hand, and St. Paul behind him watch this exploit of the magician in league with the devil.

THE FALL OF SIMON MAGUS [pl. 38]. The end of the story is carved on the east face of the sixth pier. Here the two apostles witness with satisfaction the fall of the magician, head first, an expression of utter terror on his face. To the right a winged and horned devil sits watching, gleefully ready to claim his soul.

The story of Simon Magus no doubt constituted a double warning: first to the clergy, against the abuses of simony which, in spite of repeated condemnations by successive popes, was widespread in the Middle Ages; and secondly to the people at large, against the practices of witchcraft and sorcery.

The two capitals with the story of Simon Magus show many features of the style which Gislebertus developed further on the west tympanum. For example, the devil has the peculiar body of a reptile with a strange pattern of muscles and is very close in style to the devils carved on the tympanum with such a horrifying effect. St. Peter, with his huge key and draperies forming unexpected twists, is also closely related to the much more elongated figure of St. Peter on the tympanum.

The legend of Simon Magus, as known in medieval times, was as much the story of the triumph of St. Peter and St. Paul as that of the sorcerer's downfall. It is therefore understandable that the two capitals are placed in their particular position on the fifth and sixth piers. They roughly correspond with the capitals devoted to St. Peter and St. Paul on the fifth pier on the north side of the nave; no doubt all were carved within a very short time.

THE ANNUNCIATION TO ST. ANNE [pl. 37]. The capital on the west face of the sixth pier of the north arcade in the nave tells the story of Joachim and Anne, the aged parents of the Virgin Mary. They are not mentioned in the Gospels but their story is given in the *Protoevangelium Iacobi*.[3]

On the left side Joachim, after having been reproached by a priest in the temple for the sterility of his wife, goes to guard his flock; the pose of the figure, carrying his bundle over his shoulder, is very like that of Jacob fleeing to Mesopotamia [pl. 26]. On the opposite side an angel announces to him that his wife will give birth to a girl, whose name will be Mary. On the main face of the capital is depicted the *Annunciation to St. Anne*, under two arcades. St. Anne, seated under one arcade, raises her hands in delighted surprise. The angel stands under the second arcade, overlapping it with his long wings. As in some other capitals, the arcades were used as a means of depicting an interior, since the main scene takes place indoors; the scenes with Joachim in the open air were also put under arcades for the sake of conformity. The arches, capitals and columns forming the arcades are enriched with mouldings and other minute sculptures and there is a band of ornament below the abacus, very similar to that in the *Three Hebrews in the Fiery Furnace* [pl. 36].

THE SACRIFICE OF ISAAC [pl. 39]. This capital, on the north face of the seventh and last pier of the north arcade, was obviously carved in a hurry. There was clearly no time to remove the traces of the claw-chisel visible not only on the background, but also on almost the whole surface. Probably the building was progressing very fast and Gislebertus was already too busy carving the west doorway to be able to spare much time for the capitals of the interior.

The *Sacrifice of Isaac*, a favourite subject in Romanesque art, was based on *Genesis*.[4] It was one of many representations of Old Testament subjects that were regarded as typifying events in the Gospels. Thus the *Sacrifice of Isaac* foreshadowed the Crucifixion.[5]

The scene is placed on the main face of the capital, both sides being occupied by scrolls of foliage with fruit. Abraham raises a partly-sheathed sword and bends over Isaac, who, nude and submissive, is seated on a cone of leaves arranged like fish-scales, symbolising the mountain or perhaps the altar. The angel, who faces Abraham, stops the sacrifice by catching the sword with one hand, while in the other he holds a ram. This last detail is peculiar, and presumably Gislebertus's own invention, for the text of *Genesis* clearly says that Abraham found the ram 'behind him . . . caught in a thicket by his horns; and Abraham went and took the ram, and offered him up for a burnt offering in the stead of his son'.

THE NATIVITY [pl. 40]. This is carved on the westernmost capital of the north wall of the north aisle.

The whole width of the main face of the capital is taken up by the bed on which the Virgin Mary is resting. With the help of a circular support, the head of the bed

---

[1] *Acts*, VIII, 9-24.
[2] See *Dictionnaire de théologie catholique*, edited by A. Vacant, E. Mangenot and E. Amann, XIV, pt. 2, 1941, cols. 2130-40.
[3] I-VIII.

[4] XII, 1-18.
[5] See, for instance, the *Sacrifice of Isaac* used in this typological sense on the stained glass at Châlons-sur-Marne (L. Grodecki, *Vitraux de France du XIᵉ au XVIᵉ siècle*, p. 43).

is raised and consequently the line of the bed is not horizontal but slightly sloping. This diagonal accent is further increased by the position of the upper part of the body and the head of the Virgin, thus adding to the liveliness of the composition. The gesture of the Virgin's hand, stretched towards her Child, who is being bathed in a font-like basin, provides an optical as well as a psychological link between her and the group to the right. This consists of two nimbed women, one in attendance, the other bathing the new-born Jesus. To the left of the Virgin is St. Joseph seated in meditation on a curiously shaped chair.

In the centre of the main face of the capital is a large flower such as appears on many other of Gislebertus's capitals, and below the abacus is a band of smaller flowers. In a recent study of foliage sculpture in Burgundy, Mlle. Denise Jalabert, in describing this capital, stated:[1] 'Here, by filling in the empty space with a charming flower, the sculptor no doubt wanted to make an allusion to a phrase of St. Bernard about the Nativity: the flower (Jesus) was born of a flower (the Virgin) in a flower (Nazareth signifies flower), in the season of flowers (the Annunciation took place in the spring). For the same reason, no doubt, the abacus is enriched with an enchanting row of flowers'. It is, however, very doubtful whether Gislebertus had any such allegory in mind, for he used similar decorative devices on several other capitals.

The iconography of this capital, especially the scene of the bathing of the Child, is based on Byzantine sources. Also, the position of St. Joseph to the left of the main scene is usual in Byzantine art.[2] In comparison with the subtle scene at Autun, the *Nativity* on the south tympanum at Vézelay seems prosaic, even despite the fact that this capital at Autun shows numerous traces of being put into position without having been completely finished.

THE BODY OF ST. VINCENT GUARDED BY RAVENS [pl. 41]. St. Vincent was the proto-martyr of Spain and like St. Stephen, whose martyrdom is depicted on another capital [pl. 25], was a deacon. He was put to death during the persecutions of Diocletian and, according to later legends, his body was thrown out to be devoured by wild beasts but was defended by a gigantic raven.

The capital shows the nude body of the dead saint guarded by two large birds, each keeping at bay a wild animal, perhaps a wolf and a bear. All the remaining surface is filled in with leaves and fruit on long stalks.

There is nothing surprising in this choice of subject. St. Vincent was widely venerated in Burgundy. He was the patron saint of the cathedral at Mâcon and many other churches. At Vézelay an altar was dedicated to him and at Autun, one of the Gothic chapels.[3] On the

well-known altar at Avenas (Rhône) he is represented receiving a model of the church from 'Rex Ludovicus' [pl. ©2].[4]

GRIFFON [pl. 42]. The griffon, part-eagle, part-lion, was regarded as an evil force and is shown here trampling on a man who, though lying on his back, pierces the monster with his sword. The griffon's claws grip the man's head, whose expression of agonised pain is carved with masterly expressiveness.[5]

Though placed on the west face of the seventh and last pier on the south side, this capital in its subject matter—the allegorical struggle between Good and Evil—belongs to the group in the south aisle of the choir [pls. 7, 8, 9 and 24].

DEVIL AND SNAKE [pl. 43]. Two capitals set against the west wall of the church are both closely connected with the tympanum. In fact they could easily have been employed on the tympanum, among the scenes of hell.

The first capital, on the north side, shows a devil with a monstrous head from whose mouth emerges a snake. The devil grips the snake with one hand, while with the other he holds his own tail or perhaps the tail of the snake. Professor Richard Hamann compared this capital to a relief of a demon on the façade of Angoulême Cathedral, where a snake seems to enter the head of the devil by one ear and emerges from his mouth.[6]

DEVIL WITH A FORK [pl. 44]. The corresponding capital on the south side shows a devil armed with a long curved fork, identical with that used by one of the devils on the tympanum, with which he has seized the nude figure of a damned person. The latter covers his face with both hands in despair. A monstrous animal, half-lion, half-snake, has already laid a huge paw on the man's knees.

CONFRONTED LIONS [pl. 45]. This is one of the three large capitals with figure-subjects found high up on the north side of the nave, under the springing of the vaulting. One of these, the *Annunciation* [pl. 47], has already been described. The present capital is above the sixth pier. Its composition is strictly symmetrical, the modelling summary, not far removed from the style of the earliest choir capitals. In other words it is not the style of Gislebertus and it must be attributed to one of his assistants.

The same subject, with the addition of a human figure standing to the left of the animals, is found on one of the capitals at Saulieu. If, in most cases, the Saulieu sculptures are derived from those at Autun, in this particular

---

[1] *La flore romane bourguignonne*, in *Gazette des Beaux-Arts*, 1960, p. 200.
[2] Demus, *op. cit.*, p. 266.
[3] S. Hurault, *Saint Vincent, martyr, patron des vignerons et son culte dans le diocèse de Châlons*, Châlons-sur-Marne, 1910.

[4] Deschamps, *op. cit.*, pl. 51b. The scene with the *Body of St. Vincent Guarded by Ravens* is found in a similar form to that at Autun on the relief at Basle (H. Reinhardt, *Das Basler Münster*, Basle, 1949, pl. 46).
[5] The design of the griffon is very similar to that found in the *Liber Floridus*, fol. 58 v°.
[6] Hamann, *Diana and the Snake-tongued Demon*, p. 202, pl. 1c and 11b.

instance it is hard to believe that the mediocre Autun carving could have inspired the Saulieu master. It is far more likely that both sculptors used a common model, perhaps a capital at Cluny, or a drawing in a pattern book. (See pl. ⓓ12.)

BALL-PLAYERS [pl. 46]. Describing the church in 1845, Abbé Devoucoux mentioned a capital representing 'the fall of Adam and Eve tempted by the demon'.[1] This capital is also high up in the nave, appearing over the third pier.

Abbé Devoucoux's interpretation of the subject was wrong, but his mistake is understandable. The carving represents two nude figures: that on the left is a man, the other is a woman, as we can see by the head-dress. The woman lifts a round object, which could have been mistaken for an apple, while the man holds out his hands ready to receive it. The two figures stand on familiar round supports and between their feet is a large monster's head upside down, from whose mouth springs a central flower and two branches of foliage spreading on to the sides of the capital. Abbé Devoucoux assumed that the monster's head represented the devil tempting Adam and Eve.

As we shall see, however, this scene had already been carved at Autun on the lintel of the north doorway (see p. 146), and would not have been repeated. This capital probably has no other than a purely decorative significance—an interesting representation of a game with a ball. If it had an allegorical sense for Gislebertus and his contemporaries, we have no means of identifying what this might have been.

At Vézelay, too, there is a capital on which the throwing of balls is involved, but there the balls are probably stone ones and the scene one of combat rather than sport.[3]

The capitals of the west doorways

Each of the three arches of the central doorway is supported at either end by a capital and a round column and, in addition, the lintel rests on large square capitals which are placed over fluted door jambs. Thus, on either side of the doorway, there are four carved capitals. There is a further capital, over the trumeau. This, like all those over the door jambs, is a 19th-century copy; the originals were too damaged to be left *in situ* but fortunately they have been preserved. (See pl. B, and plans I, II.)

Starting from the extreme left, the capital [pl. 51*a*] under the zodiac arch illustrates Aesop's fable of the *Wolf and the Crane*. The wolf, having a bone stuck in his throat, implored all animals to help him to get it out and hinted at a handsome reward. But they all refused until a crane took pity on him, put his head down the wolf's throat and removed the bone. Then, modestly, he reminded the wolf about the promised reward. 'Ungrateful creature', exclaimed the wolf, 'to ask any other reward than that you have put your head into a wolf's jaws and brought it safe out again!' The fable, while stigmatising ingratitude, also points a moral to those who are charitable only in the hope of a return. The parallel between this and the corresponding capital on the other side [pl. 52*c*, described below], where St. Jerome, out of goodness of heart, removes a thorn from a lion's paw, to be rewarded subsequently by the animal's affection, was probably not unintentional.

Fables were often used by the artists of the Middle Ages[2] for their comic effect but there is very little in Gislebertus's work that is humorous. There is little doubt that Gislebertus wished to convey a moral message in his sculpture; in fact, he was closer in spirit to St. Bernard than any other sculptor of the 12th century.

The subject on the second capital [pl. 51*b*] was identified by Abbé Devoucoux as *Abraham Dismissing Hagar and Ishmael;*[4] this identification was accepted by Terret,[5] and seems correct. 'And Abraham rose up early in the morning, and took bread, and a bottle of water, and gave it unto Hagar, putting it on her shoulder, and the child, and sent her away: and they departed and wandered in the wilderness of Beer-sheba.'[6] The first figure on the right of the capital is presumably Sarah; next to her is Abraham, distinguished by a nimbus; the other two figures are those of Abraham's concubine and their child. From the earliest times, Christian commentators have seen this episode as typifying the dispensations of the Old Testament (in the person of Hagar, the bondwoman) and the New (in Sarah, the freewoman, whose child would come into his father's inheritance). The faithful entering church would thus be reminded of their status as children of God, set free by Christ's redemption from the bondage of original sin.

The subject of the third capital [pl. 51*c*]—*Six Elders of the Apocalypse*—was originally a continuation from the arch above it, where the elders of the Apocalypse were represented until the disastrous 18th-century alterations to the doorway (see p. 32). The subject was associated with representations of Christ in majesty, for the elders of the Apocalypse are described by St. John as falling down 'before him that sat on the throne . . .

---

[1] Devoucoux, *op. cit.*, p. 36.
[2] M. Jean Adhémar (*op. cit.*, p. 224) writes: 'The fable of the Wolf and the Crane was one of the most popular . . . Medieval story-tellers loved to use it as a symbol of ingratitude, to stigmatise this vice. Artists, too, often illustrated the story'.

[3] Salet, *op. cit.*, pl. 30.
[4] Devoucoux, *op. cit.*, p. 36.
[5] Terret, *Autun*, I, p. 114.
[6] *Genesis*, XXI, 14.

saying, Thou art worthy, O Lord, to receive glory and honour and power . . .'[1]

The large square capitals under the lintel are 19th-century copies of the originals, which are now in the 'Salle Capitulaire'. Both are damaged by deep holes, which were probably made to insert scaffolding when the tympanum was covered with plaster in 1766. The copies do not give any idea of the fine quality of the original carving, and are better ignored in favour of the fragments in the 'Salle Capitulaire'. The left-hand capital (pl. 48) represents a nude figure (only one leg and both hands survive) riding on a monster, half-bird and half-animal, with an enormous tail. The rider raises a club in one hand to strike the monster, while in the other he holds what appears to be the monster's beard. Abbé Terret saw a symbolic significance in this capital but such an analysis is pure conjecture.[2]

In the museum at Nevers there is a capital from the abbey of Saint-Sauveur with a strikingly similar subject and in this case the rider can be identified thanks to the inscription which reads: 'ETHIOP'.[3] The subject of the Autun capital is probably the same. Medieval artists frequently represented fabulous human races, which included the Ethiopians who were credited with having four eyes. These medieval images were based on such literary sources as the *Historia Naturalis* of Pliny and the *Collectanea Rerum Memorabilium* of Solinus, both well-known in the Middle Ages.[4] The most comprehensive representation in sculpture of the fabulous races is found at Vézelay on the arch around the main tympanum. Both there and at Autun the probable purpose of placing such subjects at the main entrance to the church was to remind the faithful that the Church is open without any discrimination to all people, however strange or exotic.

The subject on the corresponding capital on the opposite side of the doorway [pl. 49] is quite easy to identify. It is *Balaam*, riding on his ass to Balak, the king of Moab, who had asked the prophet to come and curse the Israelites arriving in his lands from Egypt. God sent an angel to stop Balaam but the prophet did not see him. 'And the ass saw the angel of the Lord standing in the way and his sword drawn in his hand.'[5] It is this moment in the narrative that is depicted here; the ass is kneeling in front of the angel, while Balaam, unaware of the angel's presence, urges the animal on with his stick. It is not difficult to understand why this subject was selected for this particular place. It was clearly intended as a warning to the faithful, as they were about to enter the church, to be more receptive to the Lord's words than was Balaam when he undertook his journey.

The same subject was carved on interior capitals of two other Burgundian churches: Saulieu [pl. ①6] and La Rochepot [pl. ①4]. In both cases, the influence of Gislebertus's work is discernible. At La Rochepot, however, the angel is placed so awkwardly that he gives the impression of leading Balaam and not of stopping him. Though the scene at Saulieu is reversed, it must, for various reasons, be considered a copy of the Autun capital (see p. 176).

The present trumeau and the capital above it were carved in 1863.[6] The principal figure on the trumeau is St. Lazarus as bishop of Marseilles and on either side of him are his sisters, St. Mary Magdalen and St. Martha. We know from the document of 1482 that these figures were carved on the original trumeau,[7] though it is doubtful whether any traces of it survived the disastrous alterations of 1766 to guide the 19th-century sculptor.

We know that the Cluny doorway, dating from about 1115, had no trumeau. On the other hand, both at Vézelay, between 1125 and 1130, and at Moissac shortly before 1130, large trumeaux enriched with sculpture were used. At Autun, both the north and the west doorways had trumeaux. It is probable that the idea of dividing the doorway in two with the help of a trumeau was dictated by the necessity of supporting the large tympanum at its centre for the sake of safety. At the same time, the two Roman gates at Autun, the Porte d'Arroux [pl. Ⓐ7] and the Porte de Saint-André, have major openings in the form of two large arches. These examples could have contributed to the idea of dividing the main doorways of St. Lazarus in two.[8]

If the form of the Autun trumeau, when it was reconstructed in the 19th century, was based on the brief 15th-century description, the capital above it was certainly copied from the mutilated remains of the original work [pls. 50a, b]. The original capital, broken into three pieces, still exists[9] and enough relief is preserved on it to show that the copy followed its design fairly closely.[10]

---

[1] *Revelations*, IV, 10-11.

[2] Terret, *Autun*, I, p. 113.

[3] M. Anfray, *L'architecture religieuse du Nivernais au Moyen Age*, Paris, 1951, pl. XLII, 4.

[4] For the literary sources of these representations, see R. Wittkower, *Marvels of the East; a Study in the History of Monsters*, in *The Journal of the Warburg and Courtauld Institutes*, vol. V, 1942, pp. 159 *seq.*; E. Mâle, *op. cit.*, pp. 321 *seq.*; and E. J. Beer, *Die Rose der Kathedrale von Lausanne und der Kosmologische Bilderkreis des Mittelalters*, Berne, 1952, pp. 72-73.

[5] *Numbers*, XXII, 23.

[6] Terret, *Autun*, I, p. 86; he gives the name of the sculptor as M. Pascal. The same date—1863—is given in *Le Congrès Archéologique de France*, 1899, p. 5.

[7] 'In majori autem portali dicte ecclesie et in superiori parte et circa testudine eius est ystoria extremi judicii/videlicet dei existentis in throno et in circuitu eius plures ymagines angelorum/ et in inferiori parte hominum diversarum specium ad judicium resurgencium/et a parte sinistra ymagines in forma paradisi/et a parte dextra ymagines in forma inferni/et in pilari ipsius portalis sunt tres magne et antique ymagines lapidee in lapidibus dicti pilaris sculpte/una videlicet a parte anteriori dicti pilaris in forma unius episcopi mitrati designantis beatum lazarum/alie vero due a lateribus dicti pilaris existentes hinc inde in forma duarum mulierum tenencium formam duorum alabastrorum/representantium martham et mariam magdalenam sorores dicti beati lazari'. *Double de l'Enqueste et du Procès verbal touchant le Chef de Saint Lazare, commencé le Lundy 24 juin 1482*, fol. 118 r°-122 r°, quoted by Hamann, *Das Lazarusgrab in Autun*, p. 194.

[8] A suggestion that the trumeaux are derived from Coptic sources seems somewhat unconvincing (see U. Monneret de Villard, *Per la Storia del Portale romanico*, in *Medieval Studies in Memory of A. Kingsley Porter*, vol. I, Cambridge (U.S.A.) 1939, p. 120).

[9] Now in the Musée Rolin.

[10] This is confirmed by a photograph [pl. b] of the tympanum during its reconstruction. The capital can be seen *in situ*, defaced but essentially intact; it must have been broken and further damaged when it was taken down. The fragments were dispersed and were only reunited in 1960, see p. 26, n. 1.

The subject of the capital is purely decorative; it consists of *Two Atlantes* among branches of foliage, supporting the lintel which rests immediately on this capital. The motive of caryatides and atlantes is, of course, of classical origin, and it was adopted in medieval art from Roman sources.[1] The motive was particularly popular in Italian Romanesque sculpture and some French examples, notably at St. Denis, are derived from Italy. There is nothing Italian in the Autun capital and it is possible that, in this case, Gislebertus borrowed the idea directly from local classical models. He might, for instance, have been inspired by a Gallo-Roman sculpture similar to that preserved in the museum at Beaune [pl. *h*]. This type of sculpture is especially interesting for it could have served as a model not only for the capital of the trumeau but also for the trumeau itself, since it is carved on three sides with standing human figures, in the same way as Lazarus and his two sisters are placed on the trumeau at Autun. Moreover, the central figure is shown with both arms raised to support the moulded import of the pillar, thus providing a striking parallel with the *Two Atlantes* at Autun.

The remaining three capitals of the central doorway, those on the south, or right-hand, side are all carved with religious subjects, the identification of which presents no difficulties.

The first shows the *Purification of the Virgin* and the *Presentation in the Temple* [pl. 52a] as described in St. Luke's Gospel.[2] To show that the scene takes place in the temple of Jerusalem, Gislebertus carved an altar supporting a large chalice on the extreme right of the capital. In front of the altar, the old man Simeon takes the Child from St. Joseph for 'it was revealed unto him by the Holy Ghost that he should not see the death before he had seen the Lord's Christ'.[3] Behind St. Joseph stand the Virgin and two women bringing gifts; the Virgin carries two doves 'to offer a sacrifice according to that which is said in the law of the Lord'.

The figures in this scene are rather crowded together, and as if to emphasise the meaning of what is going on, Gislebertus selected certain details (the Child, the chalice and the doves) and depicted them in a size out of proportion to the rest.

The other capitals illustrate episodes from the lives of two saints: St. Eustace [pl. 52b] and St. Jerome [pl. 52c]. The first represents the moment of the *Conversion of St. Eustace* who, according to legend, was a Roman general under Hadrian. He was fond of hunting and it was during the pursuit of a stag that he had a vision: a cross of light appeared over the animal's head revealing the presence of Christ, who spoke urging him to abandon his present way of life. Eustace became a Christian and eventually met a martyr's death, together with his family. The story of his conversion was later incorporated into the legend of St. Hubert.

The scene depicted by Gislebertus contains all the details needed for its easy identification: the stag with the cross, St. Eustace praying and his horse, dog, spear and horn. The few plant motives are to suggest that the scene takes place in a forest. As on so many capitals in the interior, the sculptor employed here little round supports on which, in this case, he placed the stag and the horse.

The same subject is carved on a capital at Vézelay but treated quite differently: St. Eustace is on horseback blowing a horn and pursuing the stag.[4]

The last capital of the central doorway shows a carving of *St. Jerome*. This Father of the early Church (c. 342-420), to whom we owe the translation of the Bible into Latin, was born in Dalmatia but finally settled in Bethlehem, where he ruled a monastery and devoted his life to asceticism and study. He is usually represented in art with a lion because according to a legend, clearly derived from the story of Androcles, he removed a thorn from a lion's paw, and in gratitude the lion stayed with him, rendering all kinds of services to the monastery.

Gislebertus has selected the episode of the lion as the subject of his capital. He expresses with extraordinary simplicity the courage of the saint in performing the operation on the animal which dominates him in size, and is clearly roaring with pain. The figures are placed against a background of foliage.

Before leaving the central doorway, it is interesting to note the decorations of the columns below the capitals. The central column on either side of the doorway is plain but the others are carved with different motives of interlacing bands and foliage [pls. 51 and 52].

The side doors of the west front leading to the aisles are both extremely modest. Their tympana are plain and each is supported by a pair of plain columns. The capitals above these columns are, however, enriched with sculpture. They have, like the capitals of the main doorway, suffered much from weathering but their style is also recognisably that of Gislebertus.

The two capitals of the north doorway are decorated with the story of *David and Goliath* as described in the *Book of Samuel*.[5] On the left (north) capital [pl. 53] David advances with a large sling and the shepherd's bag into which he put 'five smooth stones out of the brook'.[6] Two large flowers fill in the surface of the capital. The rest of the story is told on the other (south) capital [pls. 54a, b]. The encounter is over: Goliath's body, headless and with arms crossed helplessly (a convention used by Gislebertus to denote a dead body; cf. Cain [pl. 18] and St. Vincent [pl. 41]), is placed diagonally across one side of the capital. The empty sheath of the Philistine reminds us of the passage: '. . . David . . . took his sword, and drew it out of the sheath thereof,

[1] Adhémar, *op. cit.*, p. 186.
[2] II, 22-35.
[3] *Luke*, II, 25.
[4] Salet, *op. cit*, no. 17, pl. 32.
[5] XVII, 12-57.
[6] *Samuel*, XVII, 40.

and slew him, and cut off his head therewith'.[1] David is shown to the right, bent under the weight of the enormous head he is carrying to Saul. As on the previous capital, the empty space, which here extends to the right of David, is covered by a plant with leaves and fruit.

The story of David and Goliath is also carved on one of the capitals at Vézelay[2] but there the composition is more ambitious and includes three episodes. Some similarity with Autun undoubtedly exists, especially in the figure of David carrying Goliath's head. This resemblance is perhaps due to a common source—in all probability, a Cluny capital.

From the earliest times Christian writers drew a parallel between David's victory over Goliath and that of Christ over the devil.[3] We can fairly assume that in choosing this subject, Gislebertus had in mind not only the story as told in the Bible but also its symbolic meaning.

The significance of the capitals of the corresponding doorway on the south side, in spite of the ingenious suggestions of Abbé Terret, is far more difficult to discover. On the left (north) capital is a youth with a raised club holding a monkey by a rope;[4] the animal sits on its hind legs and seems to submit to its trainer. Terret saw in this scene David slaying the bear, but this interpretation is clearly wrong. The other (south) capital is shaped in the form of a monstrous head, which according to Terret was intended to represent the Leviathan.[5] Since such an overwhelming majority of sculptures at Autun have

a religious or moral character, it is tempting to follow Terret in his belief that these two capitals should have some symbolic meaning. But of all the work of Gislebertus, they have the highest claim to a purely decorative interpretation. One can point out, for instance, that capitals in the form of monstrous heads exist elsewhere in conjunction with purely ornamental motives. For instance, in one of the niches on the façade of St. Nicolas at Civray (Vienne), there are two capitals so shaped[6] and obviously they could not both represent the Leviathan. The taming of an ape or bear was also frequently used as a purely decorative motive.[7]

There is still one more historiated capital on the west front, between the north and central doorways, from which springs an arcade of the porch. Unfortunately this capital is very damaged, its main (west) face being completely broken away and the south one badly mutilated. On its north face is a well-preserved scene of combat, with a warrior in mail armour and a shield thrusting a spear into the back of a fallen enemy who wears a conical helmet and a similar armour [pl. 55]. Neither of the two has a nimbus and so it is difficult to know whether this is a secular scene, an episode from the Scriptures or a symbolic representation (Virtue overcoming Vice?). Abbé Terret's identification of this scene as the combat of the Archangel Michael with Satan[8] does not seem justifiable, as the Archangel should have had wings and a nimbus. Moreover, Gislebertus always represented the devil in an unmistakable form.

Foliage capitals

The number of foliage capitals employed at Autun is very large: in the nave and aisles alone there are 128 foliage capitals of various sizes, most of which were carved by Gislebertus's assistants. This certainly applies to the fifty-six capitals of the triforium arcades and to the thirty small capitals flanking the capitals of the pilasters in the clerestory. Very few of the large capitals there are by the master himself. However, all the capitals that can be easily seen—those of the choir aisles, the nave arcade and the nave aisles—appear to be by Gislebertus. Some of the foliage capitals, those of the crossing and the adjoining piers, have been replaced by copies and the originals can be studied in a good light and at a convenient height in the 'Salle Capitulaire'; these are reproduced on pls. 58-66 (see plans V, VI).

Among the capitals, only three combine figure motifs with foliage. Two of them are found in the south aisle

while the third is in the 'Salle Capitulaire' [pl. 59]. In each case, there is either a human figure, or a human or grotesque head issuing foliage from its mouth. One capital [pl. 60] has miniature columns placed at the corners, with the foliage springing from them and graceful interlacements on the main face. A faithful imitation of this exists at Beaune while a variant of its design, without the angle-columns, appears on one of the capitals from Moûtiers-Saint-Jean [pl. ⑬7]. A capital in the museum at Troyes in Champagne also shows a very similar design.

The foliage capitals can be roughly divided into those which retain the design of their Corinthian prototypes and those which are unaffected by any classical models. In the first group there are several which use a rather stiff type of the acanthus, such as was continuously

---

[1] *Samuel*, XVII, 51.
[2] Salet, *op. cit.*, n° 50, pl. 36.
[3] For instance, St. Augustine wrote: 'Quod David prostravit Goliam, Christus est qui occidit diabolum' (*Enarrationes in Psalmos*, XXXIII, 1).
[4] The subject of this capital has been identified by H. W. Janson, *Apes and Ape Lore in the Middle Ages and the Renaissance*, London, 1952, p. 65, n. 95.
[5] Terret, *Autun*, I, p. 119.

[6] One of them is reproduced in A. K. Porter, *Romanesque Sculpture of the Pilgrimage Roads*, Boston, 1923, pl. 1126.
[7] For instance, on the plinth of the right doorway on the façade of St. Lazarus at Avallon (see M. Aubert, *La Bourgogne*, Paris, 1930, vol. II, pl. 73); and on one of the spandrels of the nave arcade in Bayeux cathedral. (J. Vallery-Radot, *La Cathédrale de Bayeux*, Paris, no date, p. 42). For an English example of the motive, see G. Zarnecki, *Early Sculpture of Ely Cathedral*, London, 1958, pl. 61.
[8] Terret, *Autun*, I, p. 86.

employed in the Brionnais in the late 11th century, and which is found on the earliest capitals of the apse. Perhaps it is permissible to attribute these capitals to the sculptor who was first responsible for the decoration of the church, but who, on the arrival of Gislebertus, was employed in a secondary capacity only. To this group belong the capitals reproduced on pls. 62 and 63.

The non-classical foliage capitals consist of a variety of leaves, fruit and branches, often enriched by beading, and always forming curving patterns of strict symmetry.

One of the characteristics of the Autun foliage is its very frequent use of a spike of flowers or fruit which Mlle. Denise Jalabert describes as an arum spadix. She writes: 'It is at Autun that the most beautiful, varied and original arum motives are to be seen. Many of them are wonderfully delicate, as if carved in ivory',[1] and she concludes: 'Gislebertus was an eminent master not only of figural but also of foliage sculpture . . . It is chiefly due to him that, of all the varied floral motives of Romanesque sculpture, those in Burgundy are the most original and the most beautiful.'[2]

[1] *op. cit.*, p. 202.
[2] *ibid.*, p. 204.

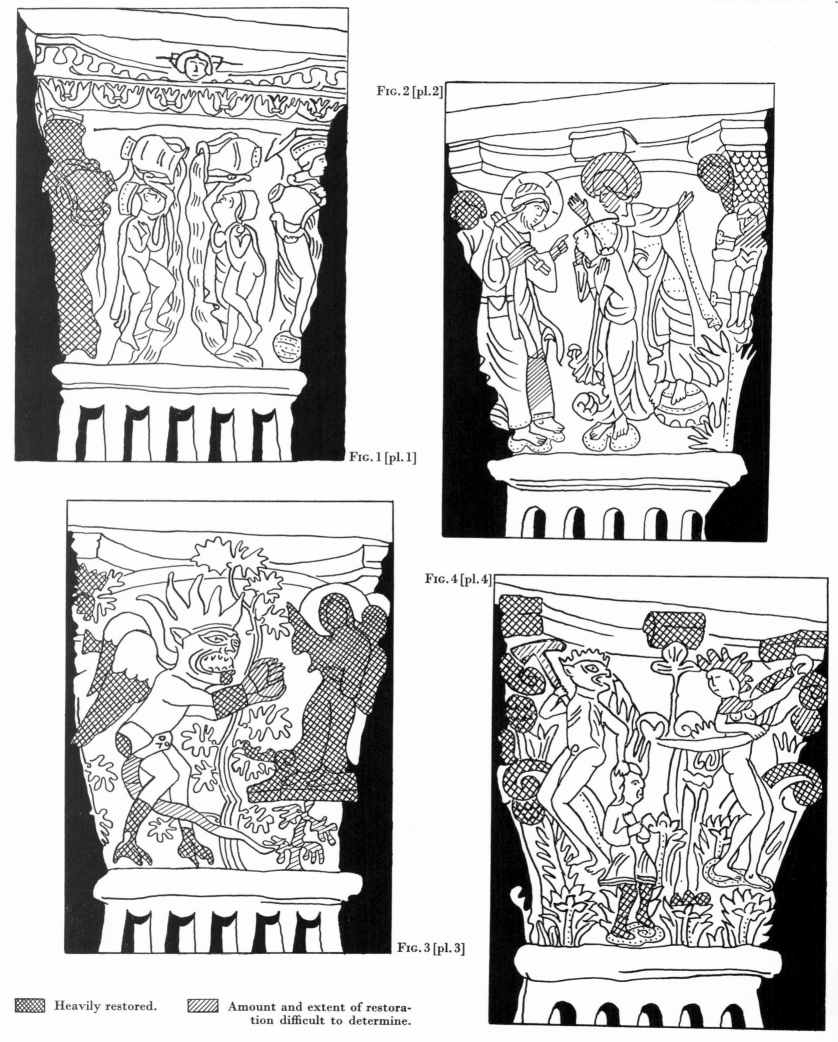

FIG. 1 [pl. 1]

FIG. 2 [pl. 2]

FIG. 3 [pl. 3]

FIG. 4 [pl. 4]

Heavily restored.   Amount and extent of restoration difficult to determine.

1

2a

2b

8

9

10a

10b

10c

93

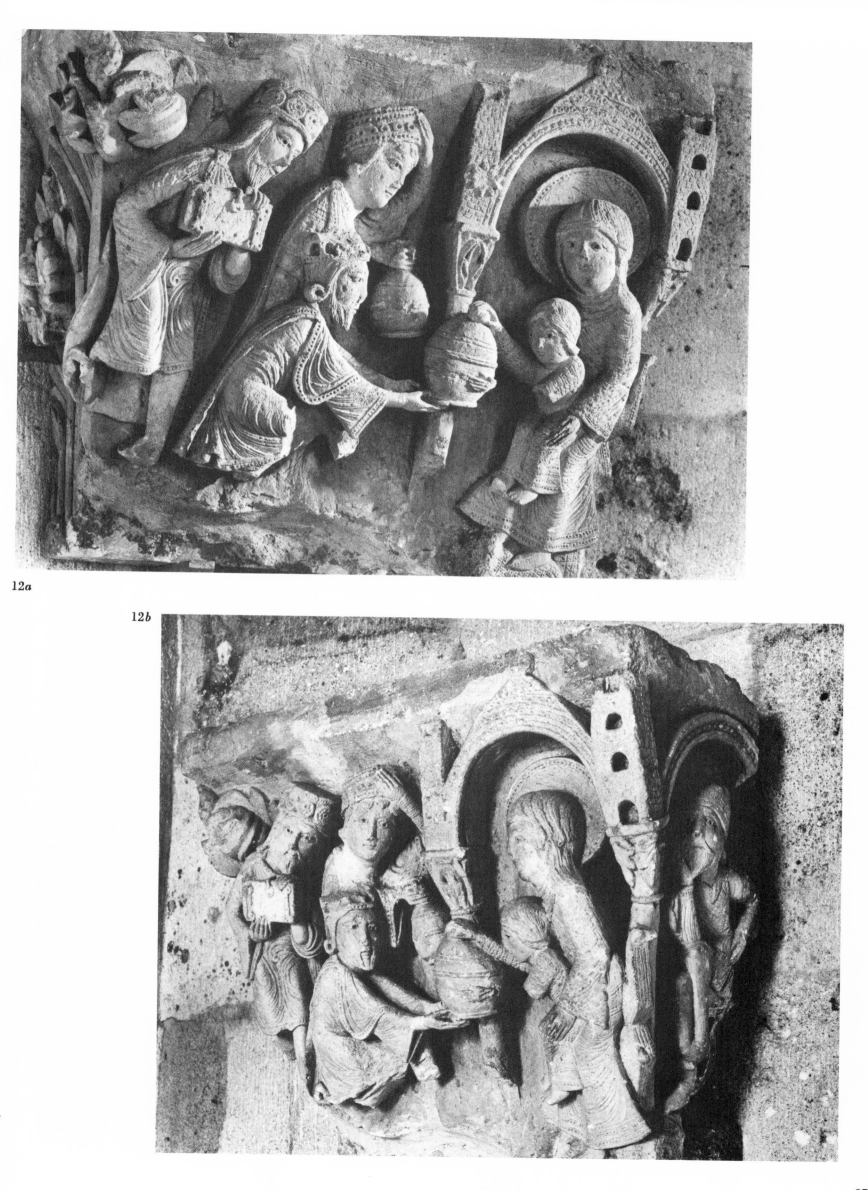

12a

12b

12c

14a

15

14b

16

17a

19b

19c

20b

20c

21b

21a

114

22*a*

22*b*

23

24

25a

25b

25c

26a

26b

26c

27b

27a

29

30

31

32a

32b

33b

33a

33c

37a

37b

40a

40b

41b

41c

41a

43

44b

42

44a

133

45

46

47

134

48

50b

50a

49

51a   51b   51c

53

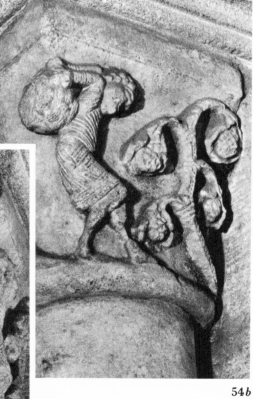

54b

54a

52 a   52 b   52 c

56

57

55

58

59

60

61

62

63

64

65

66

Plans and drawings
of the cathedral and location of the capitals

The north elevation of the nave

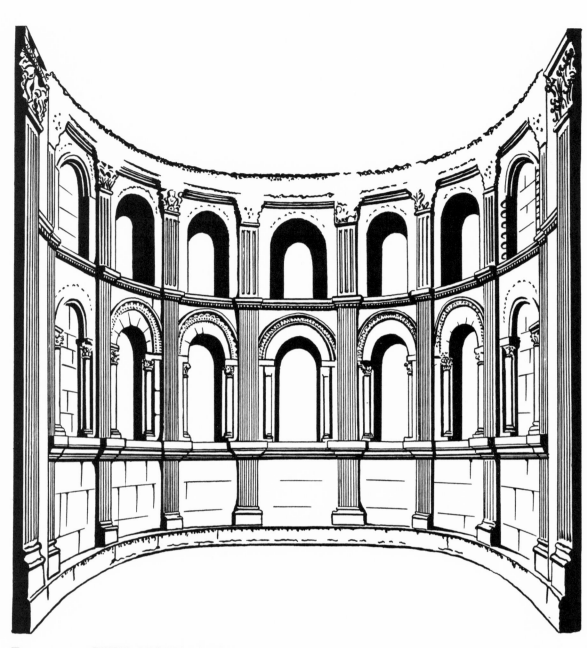

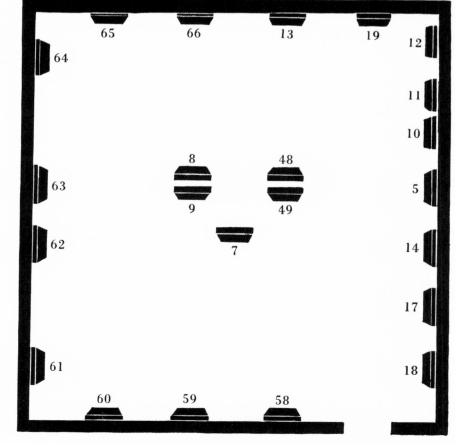

Capitals of the main apse: Ⓐ1-6
only those reproduced are
indicated

Capital in its original position   22

19th-century copy: the origi-   [12]
nal capital is in the 'Salle Capitulaire' (see plan V), or, in
the case of 50, in the Musée
Rolin.

Original position of a capital   ◇10
not copied in the 19th century, now in the 'Salle Capitulaire'

Upper-level capital: only those   ♊
reproduced are indicated

Foliage capital, not reproduced   ✳

Modern foliage capital, not   ✳✳
reproduced

PLAN IV.   THE MAIN APSE

Schematic view, showing the change of plan
while the two storeys were under construction
(see p. 57). The location of the capitals reproduced is indicated in plan VI.

The lower-storey capitals are 'Brionnais' in
style; two of them no longer exist (left blank
in the diagram). Those of the upper storey,
which are badly damaged, are by Gislebertus
(see p. 58).

PLAN V.   'SALLE CAPITULAIRE'

The cathedral museum: the original location
of these capitals is shown on plan VI.

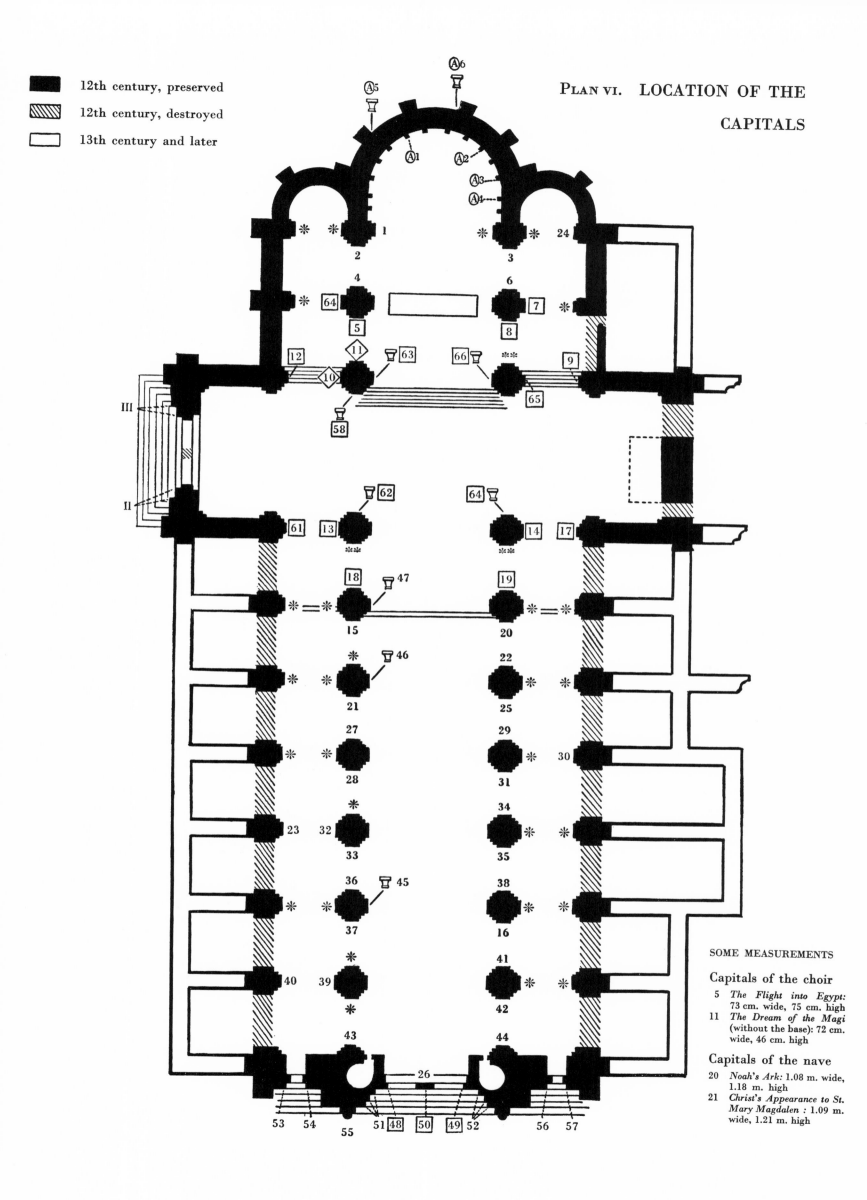

PLAN VI. LOCATION OF THE
CAPITALS

SOME MEASUREMENTS

Capitals of the choir

5 *The Flight into Egypt:*
73 cm. wide, 75 cm. high

11 *The Dream of the Magi*
(without the base): 72 cm.
wide, 46 cm. high

Capitals of the nave

20 *Noah's Ark:* 1.08 m. wide,
1.18 m. high

21 *Christ's Appearance to St.
Mary Magdalen :* 1.09 m.
wide, 1.21 m. high

The capitals

The numbers used in plan VI correspond with those of plates Ⓐ1-Ⓐ6 (between pp. 59 and 62), 1-66 (between pp. 82 and 140), and II and III (p. 157).
Numbers printed in square brackets [ ] below indicate that the original capital is in the 'Salle Capitulaire', or, in the case of 50, in the Musée Rolin; these numbers appear on the plan inside boxes, either square or lozenge-shaped. Numbers followed by a dagger † mean that the capital has been restored in stucco; see figs. 1-4, p. 82.

Foliage capitals

Plates 58-66 illustrate foliage capitals now in the 'Salle Capitulaire' (see p. 80). With the exception of 59 and 60, which were not replaced by copies in the 19th century, their original location is shown on plan VI; that of 64 is uncertain, as it was copied twice.

Pls. 58, 62, 63: Corinthian type, from the upper level and probably by an assistant of Gislebertus. Pls. 59, 60, 61, 64, 65, 66: non-classical in style, and probably by Gislebertus himself, especially the first two.

The capitals of the north doorway

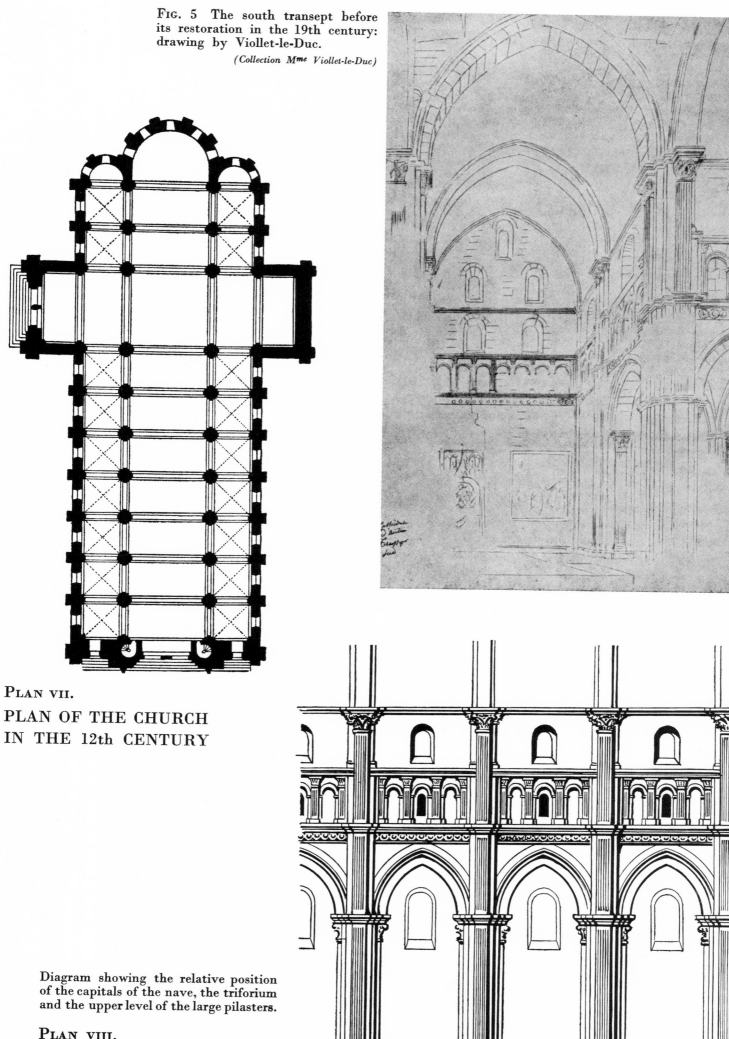

FIG. 5 The south transept before its restoration in the 19th century: drawing by Viollet-le-Duc.

(Collection Mme Viollet-le-Duc)

PLAN VII.

PLAN OF THE CHURCH
IN THE 12th CENTURY

Diagram showing the relative position
of the capitals of the nave, the triforium
and the upper level of the large pilasters.

PLAN VIII.

ELEVATION OF THE NAVE

CHAPTER 4

The doorway of the north transept

THE NORTH TRANSEPT DOORWAY was for a long time used as the principal entrance to the church since the central doorway of the west front faced the burial ground and was of secondary importance.[1]

Unfortunately, the north doorway was sadly mutilated in 1766 when, on the order of the chapter, the tympanum and the trumeau were removed. Thanks to a brief description dating from 1482 and a few fragments still surviving, it is possible to have some idea of their decoration. From this description, we learn that the tympanum was carved with large figures representing the *Raising of Lazarus*, and that below this (clearly on the lintel) were carvings of *Adam and Eve*. The entrance itself was divided in two by a trumeau at the top of which was a small figure of St. Lazarus shown as a bishop (of Marseilles) wearing a mitre; beneath him on the trumeau were other sculptures.[2]

Another description of the doorway, made before the unfortunate rebuilding, also speaks of the *Raising of Lazarus* and the transgression of Adam and Eve[3].

The only original decorations still *in situ* are one arch, and four capitals (two on either side of the doorway) with their supports.

The surviving arch is enriched with foliage decoration similar to, though simpler than, that used on the central doorway of the west front. Abbé Terret states that, on the remaining two arches (the middle and inner ones), 'figure subjects, which have almost entirely disappeared, represented angels holding musical instruments. Only two of these angels have been preserved'.[4]

Since Abbé Terret wrote these lines, the arches must have been completely restored for there are now no traces of sculpture on them.[5] One of the angels he mentioned [pl. VII] passed from his heirs to the Metropolitan Museum in New York. It is a delightful carving measuring 41.9 cm. by 58.4 cm. The object held by the angel, which Terret took to be a musical instrument, is probably a censer.

What happened to the second angel mentioned by Terret is not known, but amongst the fragments of sculpture preserved in the cathedral, there are a few small, youthful heads, which in all probability came from this doorway (see p. 32, and pl. S2). Judging by the size of the New York fragment, there were about fourteen angels on the complete arch. The main doorway of St. Lazarus at Avallon, which in many respects was inspired by Autun, gives some idea of what the Autun arch looked like when it was decorated, although at Avallon there are twenty angels.

The capitals of the north doorway under the arch which still preserves its carved foliage decoration are square in shape. They are supported also by square fluted jambs. The other pair of capitals, of the usual round form, rest on columns enriched with zig-zag and diamond-shaped patterns.

The subjects of the square capitals are closely related to each other and are easy to identify: they illustrate Christ's parable of *Dives and Lazarus* as described by St. Luke.[6] The story starts on the right-hand capital [pl. II(b)]. On the right, the rich man is feasting at his table in the company of two women, while a servant is bringing a dish. The arcades in the background signify that the scene takes place inside a house or a porch; as we have seen, this convention is frequently employed on the capitals of the interior.[7] On the left, the poor, thin beggar Lazarus, an expression of pain on his face, and holding a begging bag and a stick, asks in vain for the 'crumbs which fell from the rich man's table'. Two dogs come out of a kennel to lick his sores.

The corresponding capital [pl. III(a)] on the left (east) side of the doorway tells the second part of the parable. Both Dives and Lazarus are dead; the latter has been 'carried by the angels into Abraham's bosom', while Dives has gone to hell to be tormented by flames. From there he calls to Abraham to send Lazarus 'that he may dip the tip of his finger in water, and cool my tongue'.

The sculptor found an admirable visual form for this narrative. Abraham sits on a throne holding Lazarus to his bosom and covering him with his cloak. Dives, already seized by a fearful devil, begs Abraham for help, but Abraham with a gesture of his raised hand, recalling Dives' own gesture of dismissal in the first scene, sends him away. Alive, Lazarus is shown nude, his face deformed by pain; on the second capital, he is in glory with a nimbus around his head. The rich man, on the other hand, has lost all his splendour: the situations are reversed and it is he who is shown nude in the second scene, with an expression of fear and pain on his face.

[1] In the description of the church made in 1646, the north doorway is called 'le portail de l'entrée' (*Relation d'un voyage à Autun en 1646 par du Buisson-Aubenay*, in *Mémoires de la Société Éduenne*, nouv. série, t. 14, 1885, p. 283).
[2] 'Postmodum vero portalia dicte ecclesie visitavimus. Et primo portale quod est ad latus dicte ecclesie respiciens contra ecclesiam beati Nazarii, in quo quidem a parte superiori et in testitudine est ystoria resuscitationis dicti beati Lazari in magnis ymaginibus lapideis elevata, sub qua ystoria sunt imagines Adam et Eve, et in pallari, quod facit divisionem portarum dicti portalis, in superiori parte, est quedam parva imago in modum episcopi mitrati formata, ymaginem beati Lazari representans, sub qua sunt quedam alie ymagines modo antiquo formate.' (Manuscript belonging to the Société Éduenne and deposited in the Musée Rolin, quoted by Terret, *Autun*, II, p. 46, n. 1.)
[3] *Relation d'un voyage à Autun en 1646*, p. 283.
[4] Terret, *Autun*, II, p. 50.
[5] The first of Lallemand's two drawings of the cathedral from the north and north-west gives a false impression of the north doorway: this is shown as too deeply recessed and consisting of four or five orders.

[6] XVI, 19-31.
[7] The same convention was used at Vézelay.

The identity of Lazarus of the parable and Lazarus, *amicus Christi*, was often confused in medieval times. Not only were their names identical, but both were victims of disease and death, and thus became venerated by the sick. The sores of Lazarus, the beggar, suggested leprosy to medieval men; by association, the Lazarus raised by Christ became eventually the patron saint of lepers. At Autun, Lazarus, the beggar, is shown in heaven with a nimbus of sanctity, a sufficient proof of the veneration he received. Gislebertus included him in the decoration of this doorway, not necessarily because he himself (or the person or persons responsible for suggesting the sculptural themes) confused the two Lazaruses, but because this story fitted admirably into the iconographic scheme of the whole doorway. This scheme will become apparent when the remaining sculptures are examined.

The meaning of the other two capitals is obscure. Abbé Terret[1] and Richard Hamann[2] thought that they represented 'Lazarus Receiving the Wedding Garment in Heaven' [pl. II(a)] and 'Mary Magdalen [or Martha] Beseeching Christ to Raise her Brother Lazarus from the Dead' [pl. III(b)].

The first of these identifications seems particularly weak as it is not mentioned in the parable, and also, had it been Lazarus in heaven, he should have a nimbus, as on the previous capital. Moreover, God and angels are always represented at Autun in long robes, and in this scene the person giving the garment is dressed in a short tunic.

It seems more likely that the scene intended here is the *Prodigal Son*, for in this parable the father called to his servants: 'Bring forth the best robe, and put it on him'.[3] Moreover, if we remember that the tympanum above represented the *Raising of Lazarus*, there is a marked analogy between the two stories, since the father of the prodigal son explains in a metaphor to his elder son: 'for this thy brother was dead, and is alive again'.[4]

This capital [pl. III(b)], in spite of its damaged condition, is a delightful composition, with graceful scrolls of plants in blossom filling in the empty spaces and with a decorated band of four-leaf flowers above, under the abacus.

The last capital [pl. II(a)] shows Christ, with a cruciform nimbus, facing a kneeling woman, while behind him is a nude figure of a man with raised hands as if in prayer. Here, too, purely decorative foliage on either side of the figures and a band of ornament above are employed. Abbé Terret believed that the kneeling woman was Mary Magdalen and Professor Hamann, that she was Martha. Both, however, interpreted the nude figure as Lazarus already risen from his grave. Against this interpretation, there are two objections. It is known that the destroyed tympanum represented the *Raising of Lazarus* and there was, therefore, no need to repeat the scene again on the

capital. Secondly, no other examples of the subject exist elsewhere in which Lazarus is shown without his grave.[5] It seems possible that this scene is, in fact, an illustration of the passage in St. Luke which describes the miracle of Christ at Nain: 'Now when he came nigh to the gate of the city, behold, there was a dead man carried out, the only son of his mother, and she was a widow: and much people of the city was with her. And when the Lord saw her, he had compassion on her, and said unto her, Weep not. And he came and touched the bier: and they that bare him stood still. And he said, Young man, I say unto thee, Arise. And he that was dead sat up, and began to speak. And he delivered him to his mother.'[6]

If this interpretation is correct, it would explain the presence of the kneeling woman and the young man together in one scene, and its apparent similarity to the *Raising of Lazarus*. Moreover, when the decoration of the whole doorway is considered, a governing theme—compassion for the sick and poor—can be seen behind these four representations (the *Raising of Lazarus*, the *Widow of Nain*, the *Prodigal Son* and *Dives and Lazarus*). It seems clear that the doorway was planned with the pilgrims to Autun in mind, and especially the lepers.

From the tympanum of this doorway, a few fragments survive, and it is to be hoped that more will come to light. Abbé Terret suggested that a relief showing four feet and an ornamental band, formed part of the scene of the *Raising of Lazarus*,[7] and this is very convincing.

In the Musée Rolin there are yet other reliefs which are likely to be of the same origin. One of these [pl. IV] is unfortunately very damaged, but even so, it is still possible to decipher its meaning. It shows a nimbed figure with a sword and facing it, another figure in a pose of humility and submission. At first sight, it is tempting to think that this is the 'Sacrifice of Isaac'. But there is no trace of the angel or the ram, so this solution must be ruled out. However, since the nimbed figure holds a cloak by a round collar, it is possible to identify the scene as *St. Martin* cutting his cloak in order to give half of it to a beggar in Amiens, who was, in fact, Christ himself.[8] Although it was usual to represent St. Martin on horseback, this was by no means a rule.[9]

---

[1] Terret, *Autun*, II, p. 51.
[2] *Lazarus in Heaven*, in the *Burlington Magazine*, vol. LXIII, 1933, p. 9.
[3] *Luke*, XV, 22.
[4] *Luke*, XV, 32.

[5] Lazarus is seldom shown nude, though he emerges from his grave nude on the Hildesheim column (see G. Zarnecki, *The Chichester Reliefs*, in *The Archaeological Journal*, vol. CX, 1953, pl. XXIVa).
[6] VII, 11-15.
[7] Terret, *Autun*, II, pl. XLIX. The present whereabouts of this relief is unknown. Mlle. D. Jalabert states (*L'Ève de la cathédrale d'Autun. Sa place dans l'histoire de la sculpture romane*, in *Gazette des Beaux-Arts*, 1949, p. 260, n. 18) that the fragment is in the Metropolitan Museum of New York, but this is not so.
[8] A cloak with a similar round collar is found in the representation of St. Martin in the *St. Albans Psalter*, 53 vº, an English manuscript of the first half of the 12th century. See O. Pächt, C. R. Dodwell and F. Wormald, *op. cit.*, pl. 32b.
[9] For examples of St. Martin on foot and not on horseback, see Mâle, *op. cit.*, p. 226; A. Goldschmidt, *German Illumination, Ottonian Period*, Florence-Paris, 1928, pl. 109; G. Chenesseau, *L'Abbaye de Fleury à Saint-Benoît-sur-Loire*, Paris, 1931, Planches, pl. 22c; T. Sauvel, *Les Miracles de saint Martin*, in *Bulletin Monumental*, vol. 114, 1956, fig. 3; and G. Swarzenski, *Die Salzburger Malerei*, Leipzig, 1913, pl. LXII, p. 109.

To include St. Martin in the decoration of this doorway would be consistent with the character of the previous carvings we have discussed. It is yet another example of compassion for the poor, illustrated this time by an episode from the life of a saint who was dear to France and particularly popular in Burgundy. Émile Mâle writes about his cult: 'It is in the regions which he evangelised, in the Nivernais and especially in Burgundy, that we can expect to find representations of St. Martin. His memory has remained more alive there than anywhere else.'[1]

At Autun, the cult of this saint found expression in the dedication of a monastery to him. The abbey of St. Martin was extremely important in the 12th century, and had the closest relations with the bishops of Autun.[2]

The description of the north doorway in 1482 states that the tympanum represents the *Raising of Lazarus;* there is no mention of any other scene. It can be argued, of course, that, as the purpose of the enquiry was to ascertain whether Autun or Avallon had the authentic relics of St. Lazarus, the writer was interested only in the subjects that had some bearing on his cult. On the other hand, the document states that under the tympanum were the figures of *Adam and Eve.* Why did the document mention this subject, while omitting *St. Martin?* There are two possibilities. Either the *St. Martin* relief was not part of the doorway, or if it were, it was less conspicuous than *Adam and Eve,* and therefore less likely to attract attention. After all, of the reliefs on the trumeau below the figure of Lazarus, the document speaks only of 'other images', without specifying their subjects.[3] The description of the doorway made in 1646 is even less precise: 'On the doorway of the entrance can be seen the raising of Lazarus and the transgression of Adam and Eve, carved in relief in greyish-black stone, very gothic in style.'[4] Here the trumeau is not even mentioned, so it is not surprising if the relief of *St. Martin* did not attract the writer's attention.

Three other reliefs in the Musée Rolin, all unquestionably by Gislebertus, in all probability formed part of the original tympanum. They are each 18 cm. thick, which suggests that they all came from a single decorative scheme.

One of them is a mutilated figure (56 cm. high in its present state) of a *Youth* in a cloak with a hood [pl. VI], similar to that worn by Balaam [pl. 49] on the capital of the west doorway, and like Balaam, holding a staff. He was probably one of the witnesses of the central scene, the *Raising of Lazarus.* (See also p. 32, and pl. S5.)

Of the remaining reliefs, one is well-known [pl. V]. It was discovered in 1907 built into a house in the Place du Terreau at Autun, opposite the north doorway.[5] Émile Mâle first considered this relief to represent 'Mary

Magdalen Carried away by Angels',[6] but it was later correctly interpreted by him as the *Assumption of the Virgin.*[7] The relief measures 77 cm. by 50 cm. and being somewhat smaller than *St. Martin* (90 cm. by 61 cm.) could not have been in the same register of the tympanum.

The subject as represented here is unique. The Virgin is shown rising from her tomb, aided by two angels. A tomb of a similar form, with an arch surmounting it, is found in the scene of the Resurrection of the Dead, on the lintel of the west doorway [pl. R]. The semicircular cloth which hangs over the edge of the tomb is similar to one used in the *Dream of the Magi* [pl. 11], where it serves as a cover for the sleeping kings. The Virgin is shown in the moment of standing up, her knees still slightly bent. Her outstretched arms are supported by an angel on either side; since her body is to the right of the composition and not in the centre, one of the angels, in order to reach her, stands on a small stool. The arch in this scene is presumably intended as the vault of the sepulchre: it crosses in front of the Virgin, but it is impossible to say whether by this the sculptor meant to indicate that the Virgin's body is miraculously penetrating her funeral vault.

The relief is of exquisite beauty. The humble, yet graceful poses of the angels, the joyful gesture of the Virgin, give the composition an almost lyrical quality.

The last relief is, like that of *St. Martin*, 90 cm. high. Its original width is unknown, since the left part of the panel has been crudely cut away, leaving only 43 cm. of the relief. All that remains of the carving is a standing figure in a long, rich robe [pl. VIII]. At the top, on either side of the figure, there are the shapeless traces of two others. One of these was carved on the missing left portion of the relief, while the other must have extended on to the neighbouring stone. The hands of these mutilated figures are shown supporting the central one: there are two hands on the right, one on the shoulder and the other on the waist of the standing figure, and another hand on the left, supporting its arm. Across the right-hand side of the relief is placed a horizontal beaded bench and in front of the standing figure is a plant with acanthus leaves and a bunch of grapes.

The meaning of this scene is obscure and any attempt at its interpretation is full of difficulties. In the first place, it is uncertain whether the standing figure is a man or a woman. The wide sleeves of the form used here are worn by both sexes on sculptures of the interior capitals. There seems to be no trace of a nimbus. The first impression is that the figure is the Virgin, and the scene perhaps that of the 'Death of the Virgin' or the 'Virgin in Heaven'. In either case, there are no known parallels to such a composition in which the Virgin is shown standing, though, as the previous relief demonstrates, Gislebertus's iconography was at times highly original. A certain similarity which exists between the standing figure sup-

---

[1] Mâle, *op. cit.*, p. 226.
[2] C. Oursel, *La genèse monumentale de l'église abbatiale de Vézelay*, in *Art Studies*, 5, 1927, p. 40.
[3] See p. 146, n. 2.
[4] *Relation d'un voyage à Autun en 1646*, p. 283.
[5] *Mémoires de la Société Éduenne*, vol. 35, 1907, p. 376.

[6] *Congrès Archéologique de France*, Avallon, 1907, p. 537.
[7] Mâle, *op. cit.*, p. 216. Mâle thought that the relief was a capital but this is certainly wrong.

ported by two others and the figure of Christ supported by two angels on the tympanum of the Porte Miégeville in Saint-Sernin at Toulouse,[1] suggests that this scene, as at Toulouse, is the 'Ascension of Christ'. But this is not likely. Not only does there appear to be no nimbus around the head, but the Ascension demands, in addition, the presence of the apostles, and it is unlikely that there was enough room for them on the side of the tympanum. Moreover, it is highly improbable that a scene devoted to Christ would have been given a secondary place on the tympanum whose principal subject was the *Raising of Lazarus*. Although the lack of a nimbus is not decisive, there is a strong likelihood that the standing figure is neither the Virgin nor Christ. Perhaps the scene was one of the healing miracles of Christ, thus being closely connected with the main subject of the tympanum and the capitals below.

But there is another fragment of the north doorway which can be quite safely identified as part of the lintel, mentioned as its subject is in the descriptions both of 1482 and 1646. This fragment represents *Eve* [pls. I(a-e), and plate facing p. 8].

Abbé Terret explained, with the support of contemporary texts, the symbolic connection between the *Raising of Lazarus* and the *Fall of Adam and Eve*.[2] He pointed out that medieval writers, including Honorius Augustoduniensis,[3] interpreted the raising of Lazarus as signifying the delivery of mankind from original sin by Christ.

The *Eve* fragment was discovered in 1856 during the demolition of a house built in 1769, a few years, that is, after the lintel was removed from the north doorway,[4] and is now one of the most treasured possessions of the Musée Rolin. The relief is 72 cm. high and 32 cm. thick. It is cut straight and smooth on its left side, and was obviously supported by the trumeau at this point. Its right side is rough, and as the design indicates, a large part of the stone was broken off here. It can be roughly estimated how much is missing: the length of the stone is 1.32 m. and the total length of the lintel was about 5.06 m.; thus a simple calculation shows that to the right of *Eve* 1.21 m. of the length of the lintel is missing.

This *Eve* is one of the most beautiful and sensitive sculptures of the Romanesque period. She is shown lying on the ground, resting on her elbow and about to pick an apple from a branch heavy with fruit, a branch

that is being bent towards her by Satan. He was carved on that part of the lintel which is now missing, but his claws are still visible gripping the Tree of Knowledge. Eve does not look at the fruit; she puts her hand close to her mouth in a gesture suggesting that she is whispering to Adam, who was placed on the other half of the lintel facing her. Mlle. Jalabert rightly suggested that the curved shape of the foliage to the left of Eve's head indicates that Adam's must have been touching it.

The composition conceived by Gislebertus is as brilliant as it is unusual. No other medieval artist depicted the original sin in this way, with such daring imagination. Having to deal with the horizontal shape of the lintel, he transformed a conventional subject into something entirely new, admirably fitted to the given form. Large-scale nudes were rare in Romanesque art and certainly none shows such exquisite modelling of the body as that of the *Eve* of Gislebertus. Although he modestly covered Eve's nakedness with a vine, he had no inhibitions about carving her breasts in a way that none of his contemporaries seem to have dared to do. Her gentle head is enclosed by smooth hair falling on both her shoulders. Technically, the relief is equally brilliant: the block of stone is 32 cm. thick and the relief is cut back to the depth of 13 cm. so that the head, arms and legs of Eve are practically carved in the round. Also, some of the plants are completely detached from the background. The pupils of the eyes, originally filled in with coloured paste, are now empty. No trace of colour survives, but the sculpture was probably painted as were also the capitals of the interior of the church.

We have remarked earlier, in connection with the trumeau of the west doorway, that certain aspects of Gislebertus's art could have been inspired by Gallo-Roman monuments in Burgundy. Might this not also be true in the case of *Eve?* In view of the fact that this reclining nude figure has no parallel in medieval art but can in its general composition be compared to certain antique sculptures, such a suggestion seems justified. Compare, for instance, *Eve* with a relief in the museum at Beaune [pl. *i*]. This delightful, if not outstanding work shows a young woman reclining with rich drapery thrown over her legs, leaving the rest of her body uncovered. She rests on one arm while with the other she timidly covers her breasts. The delicate and sensuous modelling of her body contrasts sharply with the stylised, schematic drapery. The light, almost playful spirit of this work is far from the grave *Eve* of Gislebertus. And yet there are certain compositional elements common to both. Is it not, therefore, feasible that, seeing a sculpture of this type, Gislebertus conceived the idea of placing his *Eve*, the temptress, in a similar, reclining position?

From the above description, it would appear that the north doorway must have been extremely rich in its decoration and iconography. The central portion of the tympanum was occupied by the scene of the *Raising of Lazarus*, while the remaining surfaces on either side were

---

[1] P. Deschamps, *La sculpture française. Époque romane*, Paris, 1947, pl. 14.

[2] Terret, *Autun*, II, pp. 46-47.

[3] Abbé Terret's symbolic interpretation of practically all the sculpture at Autun with quotations from Honorius is, to say the least, artificial. He was under the illusion that Honorius of Autun ('Augustoduniensis') was a native of Autun, while he was, in all probability, a German from the neighbourhood of Regensburg (Ratisbon). (For a cautious account of his life, see J. de Ghellinck, *L'Essor de la littérature latine au XIIe siècle*, Brussels-Bruges-Paris, 2nd ed., 1955, p. 144). Mlle. D. Jalabert (*Gazette des Beaux-Arts*, 1949, p. 249) writes 'Honorius d'Autun, qui vit s'élever l'église Saint-Lazare . . . etc.', but there is no reason to suppose that Honorius had ever been to Autun.

[4] An excellent study of this relief has been published by Mlle. Jalabert *(op. cit.).* She concluded that *Eve* was the work of Gislebertus, dating from soon after 1130.

ADAM

SATAN

LAZARUS

PLAN IX. THE NORTH DOORWAY: A RECONSTRUCTION

Capitals and fragments of the north doorway

The numbers used in plan IX correspond with those of plates I-VIII (between pp. 152 and 159). With the exception of VII and IX, the fragments of the north doorway are in the Musée Rolin.

Fragment of the lintel

I(a-e)   EVE   [1.32 m. wide, 72 cm. high, 32 cm. thick]

Capitals

II(a)   THE WIDOW OF NAIN

II(b)   DIVES AND LAZARUS

III(a)   DIVES IN HELL, LAZARUS WITH ABRAHAM

III(b)   THE PRODIGAL SON

Fragments attributed to the tympanum and inner arch

IV   SAINT MARTIN (?)   [61 cm. wide, 90 cm. high]

V   THE ASSUMPTION OF THE VIRGIN MARY   [49 cm. wide, 78 cm. high, 18 cm. thick]

VI   YOUTH   [56 cm. high, 18 cm. thick]

VII   ANGEL   [41.9 cm. wide, 58.4 cm. high]   This is now in the Metropolitan Museum of New York, U.S.A.

VIII   HEALING MIRACLE (?)   [43 cm. wide, 90 cm. high, 18 cm. thick]

[IX   FEET   The present whereabouts of this fragment, which is not reproduced, is unknown; see p. 147, n. 7]

PLAN IX

The arch with foliage, the columns and the capitals are still in their original position. Dotted lines indicate the probable location of the door-jambs, trumeau and tympanum.

The original position of *Eve* [pl. I], *Adam, Satan* and *St. Lazarus* is known from descriptions of the north doorway made in 1482 and 1646 (see p. 146, n. 2 and 3). That of the *Angel* [pl. VII] is given by Terret (see p. 146, n. 4). The placing of the other fragments [pls. IV, V, VI, VIII, and fragment IX which is not reproduced] is purely hypothetical; though the fact that IV and VIII are the same height makes it reasonable to suppose that they belonged to the same register. The measurements of the fragments are given above.

Height of the arch at its apex: 8.64 m.

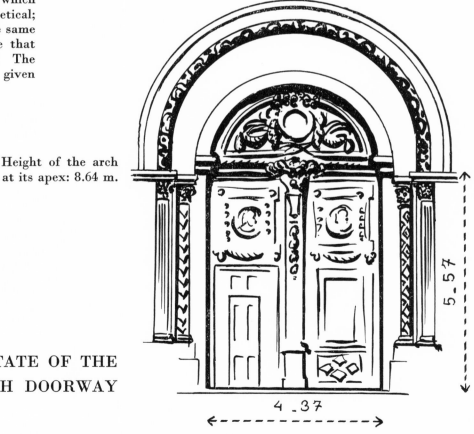

PLAN X.   PRESENT STATE OF THE NORTH DOORWAY

subdivided into three registers of uneven height. It can be assumed, though without any absolute certainty, that the register of the smaller height, the one which comprised the *Assumption of the Virgin*, was at the bottom, for, if the figures of the smaller size were placed too high, it would be difficult to see them properly.

There is one marked technical difference between the reliefs of the north tympanum and those of the west. The west tympanum is composed of twenty-nine stones arranged into three groups. The central portion is made up of five courses of stones composed alternately of three and two stones. On the central portion of the tympanum is carved Christ and the four angels. To the left and right, the remaining portions of the tympanum comprise only four courses of stones, each course being of a different height. Within each of the three areas of the tympanum, the sculpture disregards completely the joins of the stones, being carved as if the tympanum was made of three huge slabs. (See plan II, p. 30.)

The north tympanum was also made up of numerous stones, though how many is not known. Here, however, the subjects seem to have been kept within the limits of the individual stones. This certainly applies to the *Assumption of the Virgin* and *St. Martin*, each a complete subject in itself, carved on one stone. The scene which might be a *Healing Miracle*, on the other hand, must have been continued on to at least one more neighbouring stone.

The method of carving individual figures or scenes on separate blocks of stone, and then assembling them together, was very prevalent in Romanesque times. Gislebertus, while carving the north tympanum, the earlier of the two, used this method for smaller compositions, but appears to have abandoned it for the larger. By spreading his sculpture from one stone to another, he gained greater freedom in designing his compositions.

There are other differences between the north and the west tympana. The relief on the earlier of the two is less pronounced and the panel with *St. Martin* is especially flat. It seems quite understandable that, as the work progressed at Autun, Gislebertus developed a bolder technique and became completely master of his art.

The iconography of the two tympana also differs greatly. Although the *Last Judgement* consists of a number of separate scenes, they are closely connected by one clear idea, apparent at first glance. The north tympanum seems to have consisted of several subjects, but since so few of them survive, it is impossible to do more than guess at the idea linking them together. In any case, it seems almost certain that it belonged to a markedly different type from the west tympanum, being closer to such later tympana as, for instance, that at Cahors, where in addition to a large central subject, there are a number of subsidiary scenes on either side.[1]

[1] M. Aubert, *La sculpture française au Moyen Age*, Paris, 1946, p. 73.

PLS I-VIII: *Eve, and the capitals and fragments of the north doorway*

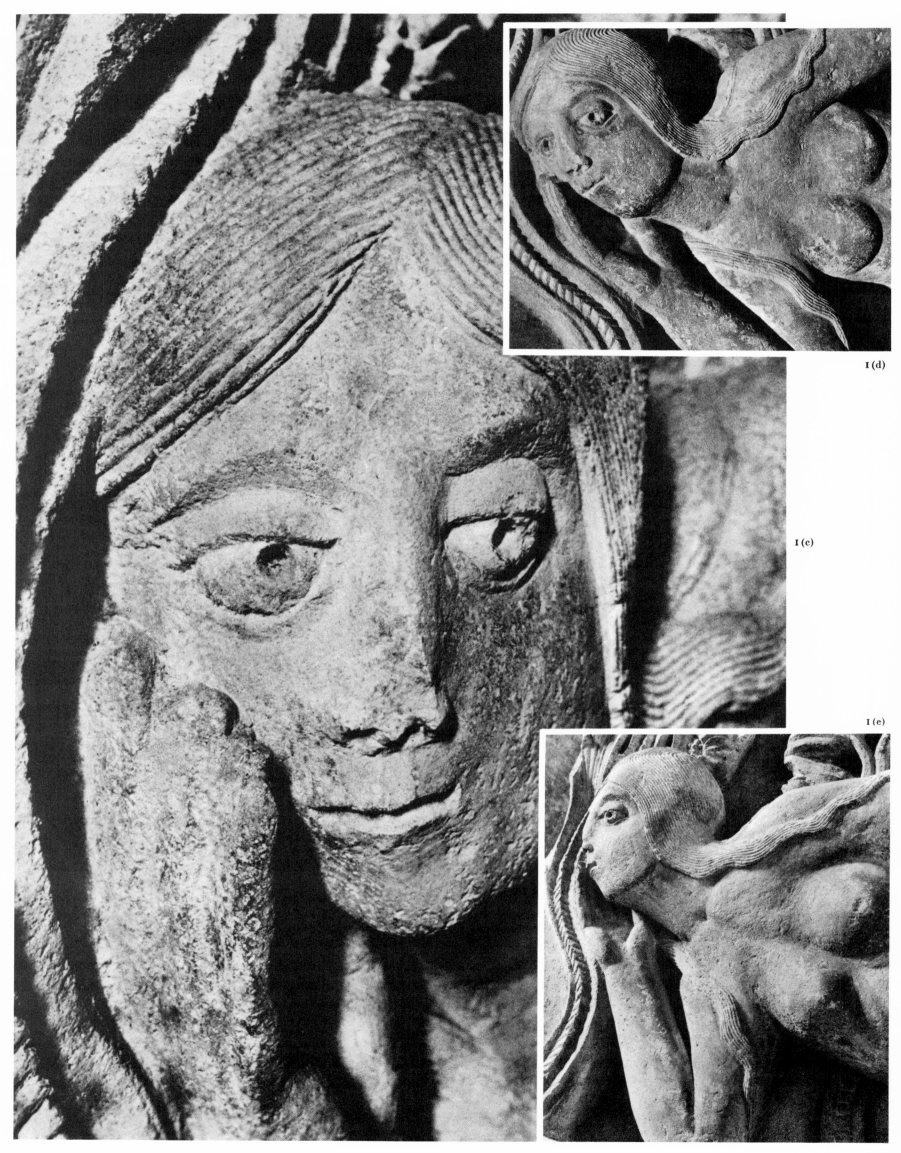

I (d)

I (c)

I (e)

IV

V

VI

VII

VIII

CHAPTER 5

Iconography

IN DESCRIBING Gislebertus's work in previous chapters, we have already had occasion to discuss both the themes which he employed and some of their sources.

Most Romanesque sculpture displays a great deal of freedom in the choice of subject. Religious and secular themes mix freely together; Christian symbols and scenes are found side by side with humorous creatures and monsters; saints, acrobats and sirens inhabit the same capitals.

At Autun religious and moral subjects greatly predominate over the secular. Nevertheless, contrary to the belief held by Abbé Terret, there is no single iconographic idea which permeates the Autun sculpture. Admittedly, the intention of the sculptor or his theological adviser was to teach and to edify. But it would be futile to search in the sculpture as a whole for a logical exposition of any particular dogma.

Most of the subjects are straightforward illustrations of biblical texts; those based on *Genesis* and on the Gospels of St. Matthew and St. Luke clearly predominate. Some of the Old Testament scenes may have been intended as allegories of the events of the New Testament. *Daniel in the Lions' Den* [pl. 27], *Samson and the Lion* [pl. 29], the *Three Hebrews in the Fiery Furnace* [pl. 36], *Jacob Wrestling with the Angel* [pl. 26], were all frequently used in medieval art as typological representations. In one case the allegorical meaning of an Old Testament subject is particularly obvious: this is the *Death of Cain* [pl. 18] which has its New Testament counterpart in the *Suicide of Judas* [pl. 17]. Both are scenes of punishment for the crimes of murder and treason. These two subjects are linked by a particularly subtle connection with a third, in which Cain and Judas loose their individuality and become allegories of the forces of evil overcome by the appropriate virtues: *Ira* and *Avaritia* defeated by *Patientia* and *Largitas* [pl. 19].

The three subjects mentioned above are placed fairly closely together. The cycle of the Infancy of Christ [pls. 5, 10, 11, 12] and the allegorical subjects in the choir are also grouped logically as near each other as possible. In certain cases, however, the subjects that clearly belong together are scattered about the building in a quite incomprehensible manner. It is, for instance, difficult to understand why the *Journey to Emmaus* [pl. 2] is not next to *Christ's Appearance to St. Mary Magdalen* [pl. 21], both of which together would make a suitable pair. The seeming disregard of chronological order in arranging the sculptures may, in some cases, be misleading; perhaps it is our own inability to discover the subtle connections between the various subjects that is at fault here. On the other hand, much Romanesque sculpture is manifestly a mixture of subjects chosen more or less at random. In

contrast to the book illuminator, who was guided in his choice of subjects by the text, the Romanesque sculptor was free from any restrictions, especially in carving capitals.

The study of the iconography of the Autun capitals leads us to conclude that their most important source must have been Cluny Abbey. This can be proved only in the case of such capitals as the *Fourth Tone of Music* [pl. 34], the *Three-Headed Bird* [pl. 8], and the *Faun and Siren* [pl. 24], (cf. pls. Ⓑ17 and Ⓑ12). But in a number of other cases there are good grounds for believing that Gislebertus used the now destroyed Cluny capitals as his models. In almost every instance of iconographic similarity between Autun and Vézelay, it can be assumed that they had a common source, and that this source was Cluny. Thus the destruction of Cluny makes any assessment of the Autun iconography extremely difficult.

Was Gislebertus then merely a copyist? We can certainly reject any such notion. Of course, many of his scenes are traditional and had been long employed in manuscript illustrations, especially in the Greek *Octateuchs*,[1] and other media. But, on the other hand, a great many of his themes are treated in a particularly ingenious way. The compositions are often novel, and there are small details introduced that seem to have been his own invention. One or two subjects are unique and testify to his originality.

The capital with the *Journey to Emmaus* [pl. 2], on which Christ is shown as a pilgrim, raises an important question. There can be little doubt that the subject as it is treated here was inspired by a mystery play, the *Peregrinus*.[2] This play achieved great popularity and was no doubt well-known in Burgundy. It was usually performed on the Monday following Easter during Vespers. The village of Emmaus was represented by some structure near the altar and the play took place in the choir.[3] Might it be, therefore, that the sculptor was not only influenced by the play in the composition of his scene and the costumes of his figures but also that he deliberately placed the capital in the choir, for it was here that the play was performed?

It is impossible to be sure to what extent liturgical plays influenced Gislebertus. However, it is striking how many scenes carved by him have their counterpart

[1] See, for instance, the illustration of Balaam [pl. Ⓓ5] in the Vatican *Octateuch*, Cod. Gr. 746, folio 31.

[2] The first to connect the iconography of the *Journey to Emmaus* with this play was Mâle (*op. cit.*, pp. 137-9) though he did not know of the examples at Autun or Moûtiers-Saint-Jean. Since the present study has been completed the problem has been discussed in detail by Dr. Otto Pächt in *The St. Albans Psalter* (in collaboration with G. R. Dodwell and F. Wormald), pp. 74 *seq.*

[3] K. Young, *The Drama of the Medieval Church*, Oxford, 1933, vol. I, pp. 451 *seq.*

in medieval church dramas. The cycle of the Infancy of Christ [pls. 5, 10, 11, 12] could well have been inspired by the *Officium Stellae* recounting the coming of the Magi to Jerusalem and Bethlehem, and performed during the feast of the Epiphany on 6th January.[1]

Other subjects, as, for instance, the *Annunciation* [pl. 47], the *Nativity* [pl. 40], the *Raising of Lazarus* (destroyed), the *Washing of the Feet* [pl. 31], *Christ's Appearance to Mary Magdalen* [pl. 21], the *Conversion of St. Paul* [pl. 32], and even Old Testament scenes such as *Daniel* [pl. 27] could all have been influenced by mystery plays. It has been suggested earlier that the 'wheels' under the donkey in the *Flight into Egypt* [pl. 5], might have been inspired by the real wheels of wooden donkeys, such as we know were used during the processions on Palm Sunday.[2]

Even the scene of the *Last Judgement* [pl. B] on the west tympanum may have owed something to contemporary drama. 'The fear inspired by the mere conception

of the Last Judgement was intensified by the Christian assurance that one could know neither the day nor the hour when it should come. This undertone of anxiety is betrayed in repeated, but unauthorised, attempts to predict the final date, and it finds rich expression in ecclesiastical eloquence and plastic art. It inevitably moved the playwrights of the Church also to present the terrifying themes of eschatology upon the stage. The number of these plays must have been considerable, if we may judge from the popularity of such subjects in the vernacular religious drama of the later Middle Ages.'[3]

Gislebertus may have drawn inspiration for his tympanum from the stage, as it was one of the few visual models open to him. No narrative composition of the *Last Judgement* on that vast scale had been attempted before. Here he displayed his full powers of originality and imagination. It is above all on the strength of his *Last Judgement* that he must rank as one of the greatest inventors of the medieval period.

[1] Young, *op. cit.*, vol. II, pp. 29 *seq.*
[2] *ibid.*, vol. I, pp. 94, pl. II.

[3] *ibid.*, vol. II, p. 361.

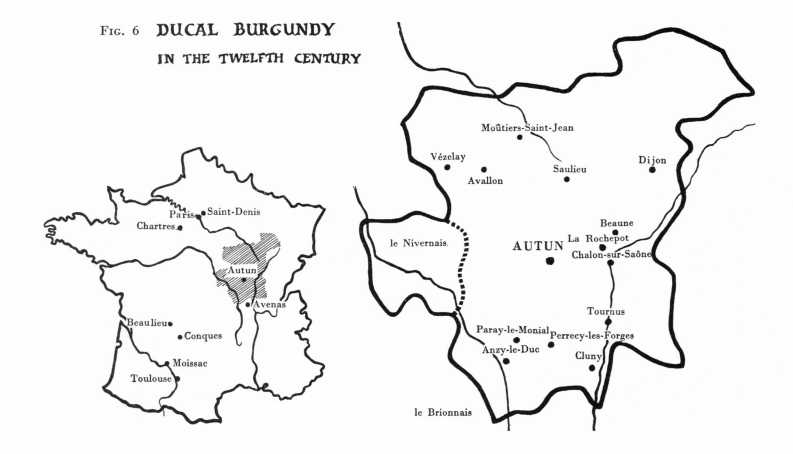

FIG. 6 **DUCAL BURGUNDY IN THE TWELFTH CENTURY**

CHAPTER 6

The career of Gislebertus, his style and influence

FROM A STUDY of the sculpture still decorating the cathedral of St. Lazarus and the surviving fragments, Gislebertus emerges as an artist of the very highest rank. Since unfortunately no documents exist to supply any information about him, it is necessary to piece together all such evidence as can be gathered from a detailed analysis of his work and of its setting, if we are to have any idea of the outlines of his artistic career.

The first important clue in our search lies in the apse, where the removal of the 18th-century marble covering of the walls in 1939 revealed new material of the greatest significance in establishing the date of Gislebertus's arrival at Autun.

From an examination of the 12th-century structure of the apse and the marked differences between its first and second storeys, it is clear that a radical change took place both in the architectural design and in the sculptural decoration when the building had reached about half its intended height. This point is discussed in detail in an earlier chapter, see p. 58.

If we are right in assuming that work on the church started in about 1120, there is a possible explanation for this dramatic change of plan: in 1125 the vault of the nave at Cluny Abbey, which had been completed only a few years before, collapsed.[1] It was intended from the start that Autun should be an imitation of Cluny, and the event of 1125 must have been a great shock to the canons. Obviously, they would have demanded the introduction of such changes as would secure the safety of their new church; and, in fact, in comparison with Cluny, St. Lazarus is a very solid building with heavy piers and thick walls. While at Cluny three windows pierce the walls of each bay, at Autun, as if to avoid weakening the walls, only one window was made; Paray-le-Monial, built on the model of Cluny but before the fall of the vaulting, retained the three-window arrangement. There can be little doubt that the reduction in the number of windows and the more solid structure of Autun were intended as a precaution against a disaster similar to that which befell Cluny.[2]

This change of plan may have involved the engagement of a new architect: it certainly brought with it a change of sculptor.

It is evident from a study of the first-storey capitals in the apse that, when work on St. Lazarus was started, the sculptor was not Gislebertus but someone trained in a style common to a great many Burgundian churches, particularly those in the Brionnais. The earliest church to have been decorated in this style is Charlieu, built before 1096. Sculpture in the same style at Vézelay dates from between 1096 and 1106,[3] and at Tournus from about 1120.[4] What is particularly striking about the various sculptures that belong to this group (some separated in time by nearly thirty years) is their uniformity—it can even be said, their monotony.

The first sculptor at Autun must have been conscious of this defect and consequently made some attempt to introduce fresh elements, especially in the foliage motives which were clearly inspired, though probably indirectly, by Cluny. But these were not sufficient to transform his style, which must have appeared to his contemporaries as extremely conservative [pls. Ⓐ1-4].

At all events, it is clear that, when the design of the church was altered and work on the apse resumed, the original sculptor was no longer in charge of the decoration. The most likely explanation is that his work was considered old-fashioned and that the interruption in building operations gave the canons an opportunity of replacing him by a new man. *It was at this stage that Gislebertus took over the sculpture of St. Lazarus, which was to occupy him for at least the next ten years.* Our certainty of this is derived from the one second-storey capital in the apse which has not been almost completely mutilated [pl. Ⓐ5]: it shows such an astonishing similarity with the figure of Christ on the west tympanum that there can be no doubt it was carved by the same man. We shall come back to this later, when discussing Gislebertus's style.

The consecration of the church took place in 1130. How far the building was advanced at that time is a matter of conjecture. What is almost certain, however, is that by then the choir and the transepts were ready, for in the charter of 1132 there is a description of the boundaries of the site which had been given by Duke Hugh II for the building of St. Lazarus. This document states that the road from the castle to the canons' cloister passed in front of the door of the church:[5] this must have been the door of the north transept, as this particular road did not pass in front of the west façade. It is interesting to note that, when the other boundaries of the site are described, no other door is mentioned, although the church is referred to as already standing and not merely being built.[6]

[1] Conant, *The Third Church at Cluny, op. cit.*, vol. II, p. 332.
[2] We owe this suggestion to M. Jean Bony to whose generous advice we greatly indebted. In spite of the solid structure of St. Lazarus, its vaulting caused some anxiety in the 13th century, when the flying buttresses were added to stop it from collapsing.
[3] Salet, *op. cit.*, p. 146.
[4] J. Vallery-Radot and V. Lassalle, *Saint-Philibert de Tournus*, Paris, 1955, p. 215, pls. 127, 128, 131, 144. Here three capitals from Anzy-le-Duc are reproduced as figs. 21-33.
[5] '. . . ex uno siquidem latere via publica est quae ab ejusdem castriporta *ante januas ecclesiae* recta extenditur usque ad claustrum canonicorum . . .' (Charmasse, *op. cit.*, p. 6).
[6] '. . . terram scilicet in qua beati Lazari ecclesia *sita est* . . .' *(ibid.)*

Mlle. Jalabert, in her article on the *Eve* from the north doorway, seemed undecided about the relative chronology of the north and west doorways. Dating the latter to soon after 1130, she adds: 'So far as the relief of Eve is concerned, it is impossible to say whether it was executed slightly before or slightly after the tympanum of the west doorway.'[1] In our view, there can be no doubt that the north doorway preceded the west and that it was built probably before 1130 and *certainly* before 1132.

If our hypothesis is correct that Gislebertus began to work in St. Lazarus around 1125, and if it can be assumed that the eastern part of the church had been completed at the time of the dedication in 1130, then there are good reasons for believing that he started work on the west tympanum soon after that event.

There are, or were, roughly fifty capitals in the nave carved by Gislebertus. Some of these bear traces of being put hurriedly into position as if the sculptor was already engaged on a different, more important work—undoubtedly that of the west tympanum. It is possible to estimate the approximate length of time needed for the carving of the capitals. According to M. Salet, six to seven days were required to carve one historiated capital in the 12th century.[2] Thus, Gislebertus could conceivably have carved the nave capitals in roughly one year. The decoration of the large and intricate west doorway was a much more difficult task, and four to five years were probably needed to complete this work. It seems, therefore, probable that by 1135 the door must have been ready and in position. Only then could the west wall have been built to its full height and the vaulting of the nave carried out. Only then, also, could the roofs have been erected and work on the interior fittings have been started. The work must have continued until 1146 when, although the porch was not ready, the solemn translation of the relics took place.

We can therefore, with a fair degree of probability, ascribe the entire work of Gislebertus at Autun to between 1125 and 1135. Amongst the capitals of the great pilasters of the nave only two are by him, the *Annunciation to St. Joseph* and the *Ball-Players* [pls. 46, 47], and it is perhaps permissible to assume that, after having finished the west tympanum and doorways, he was no longer available. Either he began work on the interior fittings, or he left St. Lazarus altogether for another task.

When Gislebertus arrived at Autun in about 1125, he was already a mature artist and his style changed very little during his stay there. It is enough to compare one of the first capitals carved by him at Autun, that with

the enthroned figure [pl. Ⓐ5] in the second storey of the apse to which we have already referred, with the Christ in Majesty of the *Last Judgement* [pl. B] which must have been one of his last works at Autun, to realise their relationship. (Incidentally, the figure of Étienne de Bâgé on his episcopal seal [pl. *l*] bears a slight but interesting resemblance to both figures;[3] see Appendix 3, p. 178.)

Although the figure on the capital is so very much smaller than that on the tympanum, it shows a striking similarity in the body structure, the draperies and their folds. The characteristic position of the legs, with the knees turned outwards, is common to both figures. It would be a mistake to think that this convention was dictated by the sculptor's inability to carve the thighs in correct perspective or by technical reasons—that is to say, because the knees could not be projected forward as this would have demanded a much higher relief and consequently a far thicker stone. All these considerations can be dismissed as incorrect. The figure of the Virgin [pl. M] on the tympanum proves that Gislebertus could, when he wanted, carve the thighs in correct perspective. A similar projection of the legs of the gigantic figure of Christ would have been technically manageable, if difficult, for the tympanum is made up of numerous pieces of stone (see plan II) and it would have been possible to use a stone for the legs considerably thicker than for the rest of the tympanum, thus saving the labour of cutting away at an enormous mass. Had the artist wished to carve the figure on the capital with the thighs projecting forwards and not sideways, this could have been done very easily. No, he evidently carved in this particular manner quite deliberately.

Henri Focillon, in his profound book, *L'art des sculpteurs romans*, remarks: 'Sculpture which is in close harmony with architecture or rather which is dictated by it, conforms in its proportions and modelling to the very shapes of the architectural members to which it is applied or for which it is a substitute'.[4] This is undoubtedly the key to the understanding of the sculpture at Autun. It was the result of the closest collaboration between the architect and the sculptor, and consequently both the sculpture and the architecture are in perfect harmony. The capital and the tympanum are not only fields for decoration but are also important architectural members. As such, they do not attempt to overstep their proper limits. Thus the tympanum, as a comparatively flat architectural member, is decorated by sculpture of an appropriate depth. Focillon was the first to observe how the sculpture of the greatest of Romanesque tympana is modelled in a most sophisticated way: the small figures are usually carved in high relief, while the large ones are flat and their modelling is achieved by graphic means. Had they also been carved in high relief, by virtue of their size this would have had to be much higher than that of the smaller figures, consequently putting the whole composition out of balance and destroying its unity.

---

[1] Jalabert, *op. cit.*, p. 274.
[2] Salet, *op. cit.*, p. 143. This estimate is confirmed by the following facts: in the summer of 1959 large, free-standing capitals were carved in S. Isidoro at León in Spain, for the reconstruction of the cloister; in their form and decoration they were based on the early Romanesque capitals of the Panteón de los Reyes. The sculptor had not been trained in any art school but was an unsophisticated local craftsman, using simple tools. According to him, once the stone was shaped to the required form, he needed one week to carve each capital.

[3] Bibliothèque Nationale casts, nos. B903 and 6466.
[4] Paris, 1931, p. 246.

PLS. Ⓑ7-Ⓓ17: *Comparative plates:*
Moûtiers-Saint-Jean (con.)—iconographical sources—the early career, style and influence of Gislebertus

B9 Autun (Gislebertus): *Presentation of the Church*

B10 Avenas: *Presentation of the Church*

B11 Fragment by Gislebertus (?) cf. the figure above, pl. B9

B8 Autun (Gislebertus): Foliage capital

B7 Moûtiers-St.-Jean: Foliage capital

Ⓑ12 Cluny: *Faun and Three-headed Bird*
(drawing by van Riesamburgh, 1814)

Ⓑ13 Autun: *Faun*
(detail of pl. 24)

Ⓑ14 Autun:
Three-headed Bird

Ⓑ16 Perrecy-les-Forges: *Faun and Three-headed Bird*

Ⓑ15 Vézelay: *Faun, Three-headed Bird and Siren*

B18 Autun: *The Fourth Tone of Music*

B17 Cluny: *The Fourth Tone of Music*

B20 Autun: *Luxuria*

B19 Venus, Cupid and Vulcan *(Liber ymaginum deorum)*; cf. the figures in pl. B20

B21 Cluny (Gislebertus?): Head

B23 Cluny (Gislebertus?): Head

B24 Autun (Gislebertus): Eve

B22 Autun (Gislebertus): Apostle

B25 Cluny: fragment of mandorla

B26 Autun: detail of mandorla (tympanum)

B27 Vézelay (Gislebertus?): mutilated tympanum of the narthex

B28 Detail of drapery, pl. B27

166

B30 Autun (Gislebertus): detail of capital, pl. 22

B29 Vézelay (Gislebertus): fragment of triangular gable, c. 1120

B31 Vézelay (Gislebertus): fragment

B32 Autun (Gislebertus): detail of capital, pl. 12

167

THE STYLE OF GISLEBERTUS
Comparative details from the tympanum (including the lintel and zodiac arch), capitals and north doorway

Gestures

ⒸⒸ1a   Angel raising a sword (lintel, pl. Q)

Ⓒ1b   Abraham raising a sword (cap., pl. 39)

Ⓒ2a   Lost soul (lintel, pl. P)

Ⓒ2b   Ira (cap., pl. 19)

Ⓒ2c   Simon Magus (cap., pl. 38)

Heads

Ⓒ3a   Pilgrim (lintel, pl. Q)

Ⓒ3b   Duke Hugh II? (cap., pl. 13)

Ⓒ3c   Tubalcain (cap., pl. 18)

Headgear

Ⓒ4a   Giant bird (cap., pl. 7)

Ⓒ4b   Raven's wing (cap., pl. 41)

Ⓒ4c   Game-cocks (cap., pl. 23)

Plumage

C 5a January (zodiac, pl. O5)

C 5b Youth (north door, pl. VI)

Weave of cloth

C 5c Jacob (cap., pl. 26)

C 6a Devil (cap., pl. 3)

C 6b Devil (north door, pl. III)

C 6c Devil (cap., pl. 30)

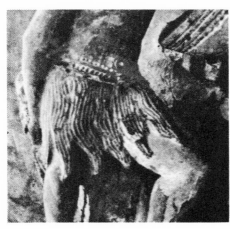

Fringe motif

C 7a Donkey's mane (cap., pl. 5)

C 7b Faun's skirt (cap., pl. 24)

C 7c Flames (cap., pl. 36)

Fringe motif

C 8a St. Michael's wings (tympanum, pl. J)

C 8b Angel's wings (cap., pl. 33)

C 8c Angel's wings (north door, pl. V)

Wings

D1 Beaune: *The Stoning of St. Stephen* (cf. pl. 25)

D2 Beaune: *Noah's Ark* (cf. pl. 20)

D3 Beaune: *The Tree of Jesse* (cf. pl. 15)

D4 La Rochepot: *Balaam* (cf. pl. 49)

D6 Saulieu: *Balaam* (cf. pl. 49)

D5 *Balaam (Octateuch)*

D7 Saulieu: *The First Temptation of Christ* (cf. pl. 3)

D8 Saulieu: *Christ's Appearance to St. Mary Magdalen* (cf. pl. 21)

D9 Saulieu: *The Suicide of Judas* (cf. pl. 17)

D11 Saulieu: *Cockfight* (cf. pl. 23)

D10 Saulieu: *The Flight into Egypt* (cf. pl. 5)

D12 Saulieu: *Confronted Lions* (cf. pl. 45)

D14 Autun: *The Annunciation to St. Anne*

D13 Carrières-St.-Denis: *The Annunciation*

D16 Autun: *The Virgin Enthroned*

D17 Carrières-St.-Denis: *Virgin and Child*

D15 Autun (school of Gislebertus): *Virgin and Child*

The relative flatness of the enthroned figure on the apse capital at Autun is dictated by the desire to preserve the flat form of the pilaster capital. The flatness, the almost concave form of the Christ on the tympanum, achieves the miraculous result that this gigantic figure is in perfect harmony with even the smallest figure of the tympanum and its lintel.

When Gislebertus carved the now damaged apse capital, he already had the knowledge, acquired or instinctive, of modelling the relief with the help of rounded forms as well as by purely linear means. The torso of the figure is in high relief and the legs are also round under the covering robe. But they are in the same plane as the torso, and in order to give them roundness, the robe between the legs is concave and the figure is placed on a throne that curves inwards into the depth of the capital. The feet, instead of being turned outwards as they anatomically should, point down, thus avoiding the grotesque appearance they would otherwise have. The roundness of the body is further emphasized by the lines of the hems and folds, and by numerous parallel lines incised and in relief, grouped in bands. Each of them catches the light, throwing a shadow and thus conducting the eye in the desired direction.

The identical system is used for the Christ on the tympanum where, because of the size of the figure, it is much more clearly visible [pls. H, I]. The incised lines are grouped, five to ten at a time, in broad bands, of which there are separate systems on the breast and each arm that help to give these comparatively flat forms an illusion of roundness. The lower part of the figure obviously presented a far greater difficulty, and here the bands do not achieve the illusion of roundness so successfully [pls. F, G]. But they provide a wonderful pattern of parallel and intersecting light and dark lines, that direct the eyes of the spectator upwards to the arms and the head. The position of the legs, with their knees set so widely apart and the feet brought close together, meant that optically the figure had only a slight support. This was remedied by the addition on either side of the legs of folds which broaden the figure sufficiently to give it a steady base.

The similarity in the treatment of the earliest and the last works of Gislebertus at Autun suggests that the span of time between them could not have been very great, for otherwise his style would undoubtedly have changed; no artist remains static.

In stating that Gislebertus's style changed little in the ten years approximately during which he worked at Autun, it must be admitted that there are differences, sometimes great differences, between individual capitals. Some were done hurriedly, and lack the fine detail and finish of the majority. It has already been pointed out that the unfinished capitals [pls. 30, 32, 36, 39, 40] are found near the west end of the nave and the obvious inference is that Gislebertus was, at that stage of the building, preoccupied with the west doorway and could not give the same attention to the interior capitals as he

had done earlier. It is possible that, since all the capitals were originally painted over, the differences between the finished and partially finished works were less noticeable at the time. Some of the capitals of the choir have been repaired with stucco [pls. 1, 2, 3, 4] and these restorations give them an aspect foreign to Gislebertus's style. One must, therefore, beware of using them to form a judgement about this.

The capitals of the exterior [pls. 48-57, II-III] may at first glance appear somewhat different to those of the interior. They are, of course, of a different shape and proportions and thus demanded a different treatment. They have also been exposed to changes of climate and have suffered from weathering. Some may have been slightly re-touched; for instance, the state of preservation of the capitals on the doorway of the north transept is suspiciously uneven. The capitals of the side doorways of the west front were clearly considered the least important and received only a very modest decoration.

On most capitals, foliage plays a prominent part, on others it is absent. In some cases, but not all, the eyes are drilled and were filled in with paste. There are many instances of such differences, but they do not follow any logical pattern. When, however, all these works are examined in detail, they reveal, in spite of their differences, the same fundamental characteristics of Gislebertus's style and must be accepted as his work.

A comparative study of the details of the tympanum, the capitals and the fragments of the north doorway confirms this conclusion. With the help of photographs it is possible to make something of a vocabulary of the forms used by Gislebertus. One can, for instance, identify a host of details, such as angels' wings, heads of devils, costumes and drapery, hair-styles, foliage, and—even more telling—gestures and expressions [pls. ©1-©8]. These details are not merely similar but often even identical and are found in every part of the church. They make it impossible to doubt that the work as a whole was executed by one artist, and probably in a comparatively short space of time.

Technically, of course, the west tympanum is Gislebertus's boldest achievement. It is perhaps in the purely technical skill displayed that the greatest difference lies between the earlier and the later works at Autun. The fragments we can attribute to the north doorway suggest that there the various subjects were carved on single stones. The capitals, too, with few exceptions, were carved from single blocks and are relatively small in size. But with the gigantic west tympanum, the design has been realised across the twenty-nine component stones, with very little regard for the joins between them. This was a difficult task, and one requiring tremendous skill.

Although the design of every work Gislebertus carved, and in particular that of the west tympanum, must have been carefully thought out and prepared, the actual process of carving was not a merely mechanical copying. Anybody familiar with Autun—with those asymmetrical faces, those strangely twisted folds, those unexpected branches of foliage, those patterns which are never regular, and above all those bodies that seem to defy the very stone from which they were created—must share the feeling that these forms owe as much to the artist's inspired improvisation as to any intellectual calculation.

As we have seen, the earliest sculpture of Gislebertus at St. Lazarus of Autun shows that when he arrived there in about 1125 he was already a mature artist with a well-formed style of his own. It is natural to ask ourselves, therefore, where he came from and where he had received his training—questions which no written documents exist to answer and which we can only hope to solve by turning to other monuments in Burgundy. An unexpected discovery leads us to Vézelay, to the great abbey church dedicated to the sister of St. Lazarus, St. Mary Magdalen.

There is, in the cathedral museum at Vézelay, the fragment of a triangular gable [pl. ⑧29] which M. Salet thinks[1] was part of the original decoration of one of the side doorways of the west front. This relief, if we accept M. Salet's identification, was made soon after the fire of the church in 1120 but was never used. In it, and in two other fragments in the same museum (one of which is reproduced at pl. ⑧31), we recognise without any shadow of doubt the style of Gislebertus. It is enough to observe the proportions of the figures, their characteristic gestures, the folds of costumes made of two or three parallel bands in relief, the structure of the heads and their modelling, the little buildings from which people look out through open arcades, the ornament of the hems of the dresses, the arcaded stool under the feet of one of the figures and other characteristic details, to be convinced that these works were carved by Gislebertus himself. The style of these fragments is totally different from that of other sculptures decorating the three doorways at Vézelay and from the capitals of the interior. The only conclusion which can be drawn from this undeniable fact is that Gislebertus must have worked at Vézelay soon after 1120. It will be remembered that he appeared at Autun about 1125 and thus there is a strong probability that he interrupted his work at Vézelay in order to take over the decoration of Autun.

There is yet another work at Vézelay which is tempting to connect with Gislebertus. This is a mutilated tympanum [pl. ⑧27] now standing against the south wall of the church, which was originally carved with the seated figure of Christ within a mandorla supported by flying angels. The shape of the tympanum is unusual, for it has a rectangular projection at its apex for the head of Christ; the same shape was later adopted by the sculptor of the main tympanum—the 'Master of the Tympanum'—whom M. Salet identifies as the chief sculptor of Cluny.[2] In spite of the very damaged condition of the discarded tympanum it is possible to see on it the outlines of the

original figures. The striking position of Christ's knees, each turning outwards, is the same as on the Autun tympanum (but unlike that on the main Vézelay tympanum where Christ's knees are brought together on the right side). Furthermore, the two details of the draperies [pl. ⑧28], mercifully spared when the sculpture was cut away because they were flat, show the unmistakable characteristics of Gislebertus's style.

Until the 19th-century restoration of the façade of Vézelay, this tympanum was over the main doorway of the narthex, built about 1140.[3] If we accept this tympanum as designed from the start for the narthex, then we have to assume that Gislebertus returned to Vézelay after having finished his work at Autun. Such a hypothesis is supported by the style of certain capitals of the narthex, which are clearly influenced by Gislebertus and have nothing in common with the style of the Master of the Tympanum.[4]

However, the flatness of the relief on the discarded tympanum speaks in favour of another possibility. When Gislebertus began his work at Vézelay soon after 1120, he could have carved this tympanum for the main doorway of the church. The church was still being built and the west end had not been reached by the time Gislebertus left for Autun. When, some years later, the building was sufficiently well advanced, a new sculptor, the Master of the Tympanum, was put in charge of carving the decoration of the three doorways. He probably planned at first to incorporate the reliefs prepared by Gislebertus, but eventually changed his mind and left them out. This would perhaps explain certain changes of design visible in his central doorway. The tympanum of Gislebertus might then have been used some twenty years after it was carved, over the doorway of the narthex.[5]

The discovery of Gislebertus's association with Vézelay between 1120 and 1125 takes us a step nearer to the problem of his early training. The very close links which existed between Vézelay and Cluny offer a tempting possibility. Was Gislebertus in any way connected with the decoration of Cluny, which at the time of his appearance at Vézelay was largely finished? The study of Gislebertus's work at Autun, which discloses the artist's indebtedness to Cluny in so many varied ways, seems to confirm such a possibility. If Gislebertus was working, and perhaps being trained, in the workshop which was engaged from about 1090 on the decoration of Cluny, he was the only sculptor of that workshop who, although absorbing a tremendous amount from its style, evolved an individual manner unlike any of his Burgundian contemporaries. For although it is possible to enumerate

---

[1] Salet, op. cit., pp. 47-48.
[2] ibid., p. 166.

[3] M. Salet (op. cit., p. 194) describing this tympanum makes no comments about its style. Hamann (Das Lazarusgrab in Autun, p. 293, Abb. 181 and 183) on the other hand, points out the connection with Autun but dates the tympanum much too early, c. 1100.
[4] Especially capitals 36 and 37 (Salet, op. cit., pl. 46).
[5] In the French edition of this book published in 1960 it was suggested that this tympanum dates from c. 1140, but Dr. Zarnecki, whose point this was, has since reconsidered the problem. In reaching his present views, he was greatly helped by numerous discussions on the subject with Dr. Willibald Sauerländer, to whom he is greatly indebted.

many features of his sculpture which he clearly derived from Cluny, he seems to have been little affected by the characteristic Cluny folds, cut with sharp-edged lines. His folds are composed of two or more parallel bands in relief. Only in modelling the figure of Christ on the west tympanum did he combine this method with that of Cluny.

That he had an intimate knowledge of the Cluny sculpture is beyond doubt. Attention has already been drawn to some cases of undisputed dependence on Cluny in the iconography of the Autun capitals. In many other instances, such a dependence can be deduced. In style too, many characteristics of Gislebertus's sculpture have their roots in the decoration of the great abbey. The fluttering draperies certainly rank high amongst those characteristics.[1] There are also some very striking similarities of detail. For instance, the ornament of the mandorla around Christ on the west tympanum at Autun, is identical with that on the mandorla of the great portal at Cluny [pl. Ⓑ25].[2] There is even an interesting comparison to be made between a surviving head from the Cluny tympanum and the *Eve* of Autun [pls. Ⓑ23, Ⓑ24]. In foliage sculpture, although Gislebertus evolved a style of his own, his dependence on Cluny models is also striking: the long, interlacing branches, so frequently used at Autun, have their prototypes at Cluny.[3] Considering that our knowledge of the Abbey is based only on the

small part of the building which still survives and on some excavated fragments, the close relationship between it and Autun that can be demonstrated with their help alone is in itself a significant proof of the debt Gislebertus owed to Cluny.

This point is of very great importance. But it seems possible to go even further and to suggest that Gislebertus took an active and even prominent part in the work of decorating the Abbey. Some of the heads (or their fragments) which formed part of the outer arch of the main doorway at Cluny were discovered during the excavations of Professor Conant.[4] They are the bearded heads of the twenty-four elders of the apocalypse re-assembled now in the Musée Ochier at Cluny [pl. Ⓑ21]. If these heads are compared with the bearded heads of the elders at Autun [pl. S6] and especially with those of the apostles on the main tympanum [pl. Ⓑ22] they reveal such analogies of style that it is difficult to doubt that they were created by the same artist. If this was really the case, then it has to be admitted that Gislebertus was, by about 1115, one of the chief assistants of the master at Cluny, responsible for some of the decoration of its west doorway. He absorbed much from the great master's style but at the same time evolved a very individual style of his own, which he developed further at Vézelay and which came to full maturity at Autun.

The influence of Gislebertus

In many respects, St. Lazarus of Autun has a unique place in the history of Romanesque sculpture. No other church possesses a decorative scheme so uniform both in its style and in its high quality. Even at Cluny, the small number of capitals which survive show marked differences in their workmanship.[5] The sculpture of Vézelay presents such stylistic differences that M. Salet distinguishes nine different sculptors who, he thinks, were responsible for the carvings.[6] At Autun, on the other hand, only two capitals in the lower level are not by Gislebertus (*Samson and the Lion*, p. 73 [pl. 29], and the *Washing of the Feet*, p. 73 [pl. 31]), and only the foliage capitals in the upper

level of the nave, which are difficult to see from the ground in detail, together with a mediocre work, *Confronted Lions* [pl. 45], were left by him to his assistants.

An improved version of the *Confronted Lions* is found amongst the capitals of St. Andoche at Saulieu. Many authors assume that this church was built before 1119,[7] while in fact all that is known about this date is that a translation of relics from the crypt to the upper church took place then. At that time, Calixtus II was passing through his native land and his visit to Saulieu was no doubt used as an opportunity for some solemn celebration.[8] Thus the year 1119 is of no precise value in dating the church. The unfortunate interpretation of this date has led most people to believe that Saulieu was older than Autun, and that Gislebertus derived many of his subjects from Saulieu. For in addition to the *Confronted Lions*, carved by one of his assistants, a number of capitals at Autun which were carved by Gislebertus himself show a striking iconographic similarity with Saulieu—but iconographic only [pls. 3, 5, 17, 21, 23, 45, 49; Ⓓ6-Ⓓ12]: the style, however, is absolutely different. The Saulieu

---

[1] A. K. Porter *(Romanesque sculpture of the Pilgrimage Roads*, pp. 110 *seq.)* attributes the fluttering draperies of Gislebertus to the influence of English illuminated manuscripts of the so-called Winchester School of the 10th and 11th centuries. This seems slightly exaggerated. The influence of this school on French manuscript paintings of the 11th and 12th centuries is now generally admitted (see J. Porcher, *L'Enluminure française*, 1959, pp. 15 *seq.*) and it is difficult to be sure, when certain features characteristic of this school are found in French sculpture, that they are based on English manuscripts rather than on their French derivatives.

[2] Fragment no. 1033 (*Speculum*, vol. VI, 1931, pl. IVb).

[3] *Speculum*, vol. IV, 1929, pl. II (c151), pl. VI (c141).

[4] For comparative purposes, heads nos. 242, 245, 246, 249 are particularly interesting (Conant, *Medieval Academy Excavations at Cluny*, in *Speculum*, vol. IV, 1959, pls. IVa and c, va and b); also no. 1050 (*ibid.*, vol. VI, 1931, pl. IIc).

[5] The two capitals, the *Sacrifice of Isaac* and *Adam and Eve*, especially the first, differ from the eight other capitals of the ambulatory. The south transept capitals also vary in style and quality from superb to almost clumsy.

[6] Salet, *op. cit.*, p. 161.

[7] Deschamps (*French Sculpture of the Romanesque Period*, p. 39) dates Saulieu to before 1119; C. Oursel (*L'Art de Bourgogne*, Paris-Grenoble, 1953, p. 60) to between 1112 and 1119; M. Aubert (*La sculpture française au Moyen Age*, Paris, 1946, p. 89) to before 1119; Porter (*op. cit.*, pp. 88 and 114) to between 1119 and 1130.

[8] Professor Crozet (*Étude sur les consécrations pontificales*, p. 39) was the first to question 1119 as the supposed date of the consecration of Saulieu.

capitals are far more plastic, their composition lacks the clarity of Autun and the foliage is of a thinner, more developed form. In other words, they are clearly later than Autun and derived from it. In copying some of the Autun capitals, however, the Saulieu sculptor did not fully understand the function of folds as a means of modelling. For him the folds were in some cases merely an enrichment of the surface with a meaningless pattern. Not only are the Saulieu capitals later than Autun but they can hardly be earlier than 1135 for they include a copy of *Balaam* [pl. ⒟6] which is part of the decoration of the west front of Autun [pl. 49]. It is not without significance that the historiated capitals at Saulieu are found in the three western bays of the church, the latest to be built, a fact which is consistent with the suggestion that their sculptor had studied the capitals at Autun after the decoration there was completed. The bishop of Autun was at the same time abbot of Saulieu, so that the link between the two must have been close.[1]

Another imitator of Gislebertus carved some of the capitals of Notre-Dame at Beaune [pls. ⒟1-⒟3]; he was a naïve copyist without much originality. The capital of *Balaam* at La Rochepot [pl. ⒟4] is also a copy of Gislebertus's work, though executed by a sculptor following the stylistic traditions of Vézelay rather than of Autun. There are other works in Burgundy which show an indebtedness to Gislebertus, for instance at Chalon-sur-Saône.[2]

But by far the most interesting are the capitals from Moûtiers-Saint-Jean [pls. ⒝1, ⒝5, ⒝7]. The sculptor responsible for them must have been closely connected with Gislebertus's workshop and it has been suggested that he carved two of the capitals in St. Lazarus, *Samson and the Lion* [pl. 29] and the *Washing of the Feet* [pl. 31].

For a fuller discussion of this idea, see the descriptions in Chapter 3 of these capitals, and of the *Journey to Emmaus* [pl. 2] whose identification is supported by the Moûtiers-Saint-Jean capital illustrating the same scene [pl. ⒝1].

The abbey of Moûtiers-Saint-Jean is said to have been built by Abbot Bernard II (1109-33) and thus the capitals are usually dated as before 1133.[3] It seems, however, that the Moûtiers-Saint-Jean master was working in a comparatively minor capacity at Autun at that time and even if he left the workshop before the whole decoration of the cathedral was finished, he could hardly have left before 1131 or 1132, judging by the position of his capitals in the centre of the nave.

Also close in style to Gislebertus is another work now in the United States. This is a wooden *Virgin and Child* in the Metropolitan Museum of Art in New York, which

has a striking resemblance to the Virgin of the west tympanum. It was once the property of Abbé Terret [pl. ⒟15],[4] and came from one of the churches of Autun or the neighbourhood. This carving was obviously executed in Gislebertus's workshop at the time when St. Lazarus was being built, and quite possibly was in the cathedral itself before being removed during the disastrous changes in the 18th century.

The influence of Gislebertus was felt not only in Burgundy but also in the neighbouring regions, in the Nivernais,[5] for instance, and even further west.[6]

Sporadic but important instances of such influence are found in places separated from Burgundy by very great distances.[7] Dr. Robert Branner has recently published a beautiful fragment of a capital now in Kansas City in the United States,[8] the other portion of which is in the Louvre. This capital, together with another in the Louvre, came originally from Coulombs near Chartres. Dr. Branner rightly observed that 'the closest resemblances to the Coulombs drapery are in Burgundy, on several capitals at the Cathedral of Autun and on another from the destroyed abbey of Moûtiers-Saint-Jean'. The Coulombs capitals date from about the middle of the 12th century and could well be, as Dr. Branner suggested, by one of the masters who had previously worked at St. Denis.

A further confirmation of close relationship between Burgundy and the mid-12th-century sculpture derived from St. Denis, is found on examining the well-known relief from its dependency at Carrières-Saint-Denis (Seine-et-Oise) now in the Louvre.[9] Its figure subjects, especially the *Annunciation* and the *Virgin and Child* [pls. ⒟13, ⒟17], are so strikingly dependent on the Gislebertus style—compare, for instance, the *Annunciation to St. Anne* and the west tympanum, notably the figures of St. Peter and the Virgin, with the Louvre relief— that it becomes clear that, in the formation of style in the Ile-de-France, Autun must have played some part.

The belief that some of the elements in the sculpture of St. Denis and Chartres were of Burgundian origin has been somewhat compromised recently by a too emphatic insistence on their importance at the expense of the far more decisive influences of Languedoc and the West of France.[10] Nevertheless, the connection does exist and

---

[1] M. Pierre Quarré in a recently published lecture expressed a similar belief in the priority of Autun over Saulieu (*Les chapiteaux de Saint-Andoche de Saulieu et leurs modèles autunois*, in *Les Actes du 84e Congrès national de sociétés savantes, Dijon, 1959*, Dijon, 1961.

[2] Deschamps, *French Sculpture of the Romanesque Period*, pls. 39b-c.

[3] Plancher, *op. cit.*, I, p. 516. Porter (*Fogg Art Museum Notes*, 1922, p. 25) who first published these capitals, dated them to between 1120 and 1130.

[4] First published by Terret (*Autun*, II, p. 63 and frontispiece) and subsequently by M. B. Freeman (*A Romanesque Virgin from Autun*, in *The Metropolitan Museum of Art Bulletin*, new series, vol. VIII, 1949-50, pp. 112 *seq.*).

[5] M. Anfray, *op. cit.*, Paris, 1951, p. 277.

[6] For instance, at Bommiers (Indre) the style of Autun is clearly seen in the decoration of the capitals (Deschamps, *French Sculpture of the Romanesque Period*, pl. 63b).

[7] However, Kingsley Porter's attempt to identify Gislebertus of Autun and Gilabertus of Toulouse as one person (*op. cit.*, pp. 157 *seq.*) must be emphatically rejected.

[8] *A Romanesque Capital from Coulombs*, in *The Nelson Gallery and Atkins Museum Bulletin*, January 1960, pp. 1 *seq.*

[9] M. Aubert, *French Sculpture at the Beginning of the Gothic Period, 1140-1225*, Florence-Paris, 1929, pl. 21.

[10] The exponent of this extreme view is Dr. W. S. Stoddard (*The West Portals of Saint-Denis and Chartres. Sculpture in the Ile-de-France from 1140 to 1190. Theory of Origins*, Cambridge (U.S.A.), 1952, pp. 48 *seq.*).

it is undeniable that, even at Chartres, the elongation of the column-figures, and the spiral folds and ornamental bands across the thighs of a few figures on the Portail Royal, are derived from the Autun tympanum.

It may seem strange that the influence of Autun is more evident at Chartres than at St. Denis. The explanation of this may, however, be found in the fact that, although the west doorway of Autun was ready by about 1135, it probably remained for a few years covered by the scaffolding that was necessary for the erection of the west front. Thus, the full impact of Gislebertus's masterpiece was no doubt somewhat delayed. The west front of St. Denis was decorated between 1137 and 1140, too early to benefit from Gislebertus's achievement. By the middle of the century, however, at Chartres, at Carrières-Saint-Denis and at Coulombs, the influence of Autun is already perceptible.

The prestige of St. Denis was immense, and it is significant that when, after the fire of 1137, the façade of St. Benignus in Dijon, the capital of Burgundy, was decorated, it was not Autun but St. Denis that served as a model.[1] The art of Gislebertus was the climax of Romanesque sculpture, but the immediate future lay elsewhere.

Despite this, the visionary genius of Gislebertus was not a spent force. Later in the 12th century, as well as in the next, many of his ideas passed into the currency of French sculpture. The narrative *Last Judgements* of Gothic cathedrals followed neither the example of Chartres or St. Denis, nor of Moissac, Beaulieu or Conques, but of Autun. The interceding figure of the Virgin, the picturesque motive of the weighing of souls and the angels separating the elect from the damned, became commonplace. Also, the full significance of the *Eve* of Autun was not realised for a long time. It was not until the 13th century that sculptors were able adequately to express the beauty of the human form in stone, in a way comparable to that which is embodied in Gislebertus's *Eve*. It was, above all, the plastic quality, the bold volume and astonishing originality of so much of his work that were Gislebertus's chief contribution to medieval sculpture.

[1] P. Quarré, *La sculpture des anciens portails de Saint-Bénigne de Dijon*, in *Gazette des Beaux-Arts*, 1957, pp. 177-94.

Appendixes

1. ANALYSIS OF PAINT

The *Dream of the Magi* capital is the only sculpture at Autun that still bears traces of the original colouring. Fragments of the paint were submitted for analysis to Mr. S. Rees Jones, of the Courtauld Institute, London, to whom we are indebted for the following notes:

The sample was in the form of a mixture of small flakes of paint from which it was possible to pick out specimens of a particular colour for analysis, and for inspection under the microscope; for the latter purpose the specimen was mounted in a synthetic resin and cross-sectioned.

All the samples were found to have a layer of yellow ochre paint under the surface layer. The following are the pigments used in the final layer:

> *red*—iron oxide earth;
> *blue*—azurite;
> *yellow*—ochre;
> *white*—white lead.

The presence of medium indicated that the technique was not fresco or lime wash but it was not found possible to determine its nature precisely. The paint film strongly resists water and common organic solvents such as acetone and alcohol. The probability is that the medium is some form of emulsion.

2. THE OPPÉ RELIEF

A small fragment of a relief 30 cm. high and 9 cm. thick [pl. Ⓑ11], in the collection of Miss A. Oppé, London, shows very striking similarities with the figure of the layman—probably that of Duke Hugh II—on the capital of the *Presentation of the Church* [pl. Ⓑ9]. It appears, in fact, to be a smaller version of this figure, the only difference being that the object carried is a book and not a model of the church.

The London relief comes from the well-known collection of the late Alphonse Kann (it was sold at Sotheby's on 9th March 1956 as lot 66) and seems, on examination, to be perfectly genuine. To establish its authenticity beyond question, however, it would be necessary to take it to Autun for a minute comparison of the stone and the peculiarities of style.

If the fragment is an authentic work of Gislebertus, then it must have been made at the same time as the capital, though for what purpose is a matter for speculation. The figure of the Duke on the relief is smaller than that on the capital so it is not part of a capital which was accidentally broken and immediately replaced by Gislebertus with another version of the same subject. Moreover, the relief is thinner than the Autun capitals. It is not a first model, for Gislebertus's sculptures show such freedom and improvisation in the treatment of forms that it is clear he used no models (except perhaps sketches in his pattern book). It is more likely that the Duke, pleased with the capital on which he was represented, commissioned another work—reredos, screen or some other church fitting—to be carved at his expense and to show a similar figure of himself; in this instance, the model of the church on the capital was replaced by a book. This explanation is, of course, a pure conjecture.

3. SEAL OF ÉTIENNE DE BÂGÉ

The seal of Étienne de Bâgé, bishop of Autun at the time of the building of St. Lazarus, shows him seated in exactly the same position, with the knees turned outwards, as Christ on the apse capital and on the tympanum [pls. Ⓐ5, *l* and *m*].

The seal is too small and indistinct to justify any claim that it is by Gislebertus, though this cannot be ruled out. Many artists of this period worked in more than one technique, for example Magister Hugo, a secular artist, who was active at Bury St. Edmunds during the abbacy of Anselm (d. 1148). Hugo not only illuminated the celebrated Bury Bible (Cambridge, Corpus Christi College, MS. 2) but also cast bronze doors and bells, and carved large figures in wood. He was probably also responsible for making the seal of the abbey of Bury St. Edmunds.[1] It would not be surprising if Gislebertus made the seal for Bishop Étienne. Some features of his style as a sculptor in stone, especially the bands of folds in relief, suggest that he was familiar with metalwork techniques.

[1] G. Zarnecki, *English Romanesque Lead Sculpture*, 1957, p. 6, pl. 8.

Index